IS THERE HOPE?

A GUIDE FOR MEN TO BECOME
CONFIDENT, GREAT LEADERS AND
AN EXAMPLE TO OTHERS. BE THE DUDE
WHO PEOPLE WANT TO FOLLOW AND
BE LIKE. THE ABILITY WITHIN YOU TO
BECOME A POSITIVE, POWERFUL FORCE
FOR GOOD AND STILL BE A BAD ASS.

BLAIR D. HOPE

IS THERE HOPE?

Copyright © 2025 Blair D. Hope

ISBN (Paperback): 979-8-89672-016-4
ISBN (Hardback): 979-8-89672-032-4
ISBN (Ebook): 979-8-89672-017-1

Printed in the United States of America.

PROMINENT
BOOKS

5830 E 2nd St, Ste 7000 #9983
Casper, WY 82609
USA

DEDICATION

To my bride Christine, the love of my life and best friend for 28 years now. Thank you for your patience and dedication to my healing journey. Thank you for catching the eye of the "wall flower."

To my children, Christian, Jonathon, Gage, Kiley, Dalton, and Bridger. Thank you for not giving up on Dad. May you ever have *Hope* in everything you do.

To my mother, Carolyn Olsen Wipperman. For never giving up on us kids. I am forever grateful to you.

CONTENTS

INTRODUCTION

Hope and confidence cause the demise of the ailments of the emotions doubt, depression, and the most fatal, suicide. Do you feel there is no Hope? Do you lack confidence? You're not alone. I was there, along with many other people.

In this book I am going to share with you how I experienced those feelings and the lack of hope and confidence, to the extreme of almost losing everything I had, my family, my bride, and my own life. But most importantly, I am going to share with you how you can have hope and regain the confidence to be the man God created you to be. The man you want to be. My trials and tribulations are mine and your trials are yours. Regardless of how small or large your trials are, you will find we are not that different from each other.

This is from a person who is familiar with the taste of gun metal, feeling that his family has abandoned him, almost losing his wife, and not knowing what he is going to do for a career. I attest to you there is a way to find hope and build or rebuild confidence. I have been there, I have felt it, I have overcome those feelings. I have experienced the lack of love, lack of acceptance, the loss of lives, and the depths of personal hell. I have overcome adversity, disability, depression, and PTSD. I have found a way to battle back, regain confidence, and realize that there is always Hope, and that I am never alone. I have become the dude that people want to follow, and you can too.

I have a passion to share what I have learned along my healing journey. This passion has led to me to writing this book to share my story, with the hope that it may cause some reflection and confirm that there is "Hope, and God gives Hope."

Who doesn't want a better life? Who doesn't want to believe that there is Hope for them? Who doesn't want to regain confidence? By realizing you have Hope, and regaining confidence, you will get your life back, your wife back, your family back, your career back!

I got my life back. I am a better man today than yesterday. I can recognize the blessings and opportunities around me. I got my wife and family back. My family now know my story, they understand and have forgiven me. We have never been closer. I got my career back as a senior executive with a fortune 500 company. I have never made more money for my family, than now. My wife and I have built our dream home on a mountain with a great view. We have never been closer in 28 years of marriage than right now. We have the opportunity and blessing of helping others. Among those learnings and blessing, my wife and I have founded "The Hope for Life Foundation," proudly serving veterans. Most importantly, I have regained the confidence and strength to tell my story. Who needs to hear your story?

I promise you, if you read this book, reflect on it, and apply the teachings it contains, you too will find that there is Hope for you. You're not alone, and you will chart a course to regaining confidence in becoming the dude who people want to follow.

Don't wait, don't turn the page, purchase this book RIGHT NOW if you haven't already. Start your healing journey. Don't let any obstacle or others from your past have anymore free rent space in your head. Regain your confidence, know that you are not alone and that there is always HOPE for YOU.

The stories and testimonies you are about to read have proven results. Each chapter provides new secrets that will help you stay in control of your life's future and get a leg up on the demons and masks competing for space in your mind. If you follow the action steps that I reveal in this book, you will enjoy the rest of your life unburdened. How does that sound? Pretty great, right?

First action step: purchase this book, the workbook, and the audio version of this book. Take it on the road during those windshield times to and from work, and long drives. Listen to it at the gym, as you're strengthening your body, strengthen your mental acuity. The audio book is read by my friend and mentor Dave Bresnahan, a fellow writer, actor, and director of movies. Dave is the editor of my book and has added priceless insights and guidance.

Please welcome Dave Bresnahan.

The workbook gives you a place to record your thoughts and formulate your personal goals. You will create a step-by-step action plan in your workbook that will bring those goals to a reality.

There is "HOPE."
God does give "HOPE."

CHAPTER 1

Hope Is Real

*"Hope is being able to see that there is
light despite all the darkness."*
—*Blair D. Hope*

To be very clear, I am nobody special. I could never change the world. Only one man can change the world, his name is Jesus.

But if the experiences that I have gone through, could have an impact on just one person, to reflect upon their life and make a positive change for the better, that would be a true success and evidence that "God does give HOPE."

If just one person can see the power of "HOPE" in their life, that Hope can rescue them from anxiety, depression, anger, shame, guilt, sadness, fear, divorce, the taste of gun metal in their mouth, and suicide.

So, I ask you "Is there "HOPE?" I will attest to you, that there is "HOPE." God gives "HOPE."

Yes, one could argue, that I am making a play on my surname "HOPE." As a matter of fact, I am. God has not only given me an awesome surname, He has shown me the power of "HOPE."

I have long desired to write this book, if for no other reason than to put my words to paper. If along the way I help one person, then surely, I have met life with success.

"Who am I?"

My name is Blair Duane Hope. I was born to William Wayne Hope and Carolyn Olsen Sargent.

My Father is from Chesterfield, Utah. He is one of seven children. He was in the Army, and we lived in Fort McClellan, Alabama, Fort Bragg, North Carolina, and Fort Lee, Virginia. My Mother is from Salt Lake City, Utah. She is one of six children.

I have come to know, after many trials and challenges, that I am a very blessed man who has had an awesome life (I have had to learn to say that and learn to realize how blessed I really am). I am a son of God, a husband, father of six children, and a grandfather of nine children. I am a disabled combat veteran who has traveled the world.

I had an interesting childhood, adulthood, military, and professional career. I have been married twice. The first marriage for three years while in the Navy, where I was blessed with two boys, Christian James Hope, and Jonathon Roth Hope. I married Amy Lynn Kulwicki when I was in the Navy. She was pregnant with another man's child when we got married. In California, when you have a child after you are married, the child can be legally yours. So, we gave CJ my last name. He is my Son, and I would challenge anybody otherwise.

I later met Christine Ann Allen at a single adult church dance. Wow, talk about a true inspiration of hope and divine intervention.

I have been married to my second wife, Christine Allen Hope, for 28 years. What an awesome woman she is, to have put up with me and all my iniquities and shortcomings. We have four children, Gage Malan Hope, Kiley Anona Hope, Dalton Blair Hope, and Bridger Williams Hope.

So you see that "God does give "HOPE." I did not want to be a Hope Statistic.

I "HOPE" to share with you my life's experiences and what I have learned in the following chapters. I would "HOPE" to share with you and have you experience the vulnerability, truth, transparency, and transformation I have gone through by improving my life. The same thing that you must do to accept the power of "HOPE" in your life.

Vulnerable: Susceptible to physical or emotional attack or harm. I cannot tell you how vulnerable I have felt in the process of dealing with my demons, and healing while having the desire to write this book. As a combat veteran who deals with PTSD, who has had to admit I need help, I had to be willing to receive help, and most importantly had to acknowledge and be willing to apply and put into action what I had learned during my therapy. (More to come in the following chapters).

Truth: The quality or state of being true. Honesty is critical. Can you bear the burden of Truth? You must be truthful and honest with yourself if you are going to receive the power of "HOPE" and allow it to enable and empower you. You must accept truth to realize where you have been, where you are, and where you want to go. You must embrace the truth to transform into a better person.

Transparency: The quality of being easily seen through, while transparency in a business or governance context refers to being open and honest. Are you transparent with yourself, your spouse, others around you? Are you ready to be honest with others? Are you willing to accept the view of others about you, not that you have to agree with them, but ask yourself, "What If?" What if what they are saying is true? How can I apply what they have said and make a difference?

Transformation: A thorough or dramatic change in form or appearance.

If you have felt vulnerable, if you have accepted the truth, if you are transparent, you are ready for transformation. True transformation is the application of what you have learned that can make you a better person, spouse, father, employee.

Proof of transformation is how well you view yourself, or just as important, how others view the transformation in you.

I really wasn't a bad kid. My life wasn't that bad, as I now look back on it. It's all a matter of perspective really. How things can change when you have a different perspective.

Just because you think your family or loved ones left you, doesn't make you a bad person. It all has to do with what's in your heart.

Hopefully throughout this book, you can reflect on what has happened to you and gain a respect and a new perspective that God does give "HOPE."

I didn't do it alone. Something, or someone, must be watching over me. God was there for me. I just had to open the door and accept his helping hand.

"There are no atheists in foxholes," as the saying goes. God does give "HOPE." We are a symbol, you and me. We give others "HOPE," when we choose to do so. This is what happens when God shows up.

There is "HOPE."
God does give "HOPE."

CHAPTER 2

Attitude Is Everything!!

"Your attitude towards life determines
life's attitude toward you."
—Blair D. Hope

Attitude is 10 percent of what happens to you, and 90 percent how you react to it. How do you choose to react to your life? Your tribulations? Your weaknesses?

Your attitude is more important than anything else. Not your past, not your education, not your circumstances, not your failures or successes, not even what other people think or say or do. Your attitude will make or break you. We have a choice, every day, regarding the attitude we embrace. We cannot change all those other things. We can only change our attitude.

"Work hard for what you want because it won't come to you without a fight. You have to be strong and courageous and know that you can do anything you put your mind to. If somebody puts you down or criticizes you, just keep on believing in yourself and turn it into something positive." - Leah LaBelle

"How am I? I'm alright so far," said the optimist as he fell past the 13th floor window.

"Remember, the thoughts that you think and the statements you make regarding yourself determine your mental attitude. If you have a worthwhile objective, find the one reason why you can achieve it rather than hundreds of reasons why you can't." - Napoleon Hill

"Darkness cannot drive out darkness, only light can do that. Hate cannot drive out hate, only love can do that." - Martin Luther King, Jr.

Have you ever been given a chance at something, and failed to take advantage of it? Did you take advantage of it? What was your attitude?

You always have time for what you want to do. You will always make time for what you want to do. Believe, do not fear.

I would like to share a couple of stories with you. The first is a story I have used many times in groups of people when explaining to them that it's all a matter of perspective.

The second is a story I share when I was reflecting on my own life during the Desert Storm War.

The Farmer's Story:

A family was driving through a community to look for a new place to call home and raise their children. When driving down the road, they came upon a farmer out working his land. They stopped and asked the farmer what he thought about the community. The farmer asked the family how the community was where they came from. The family stated that they were a bunch of back biters, cliquish, and liars. They did not like their community at all. The farmer stated it was the same way here in this community.

A second family was driving through the farmer's community and asked the same questions. The famer once again asked, "How is the community where you come from?" The family stated that it was okay. They got along with some people and some they did not get along with. The farmer stated that it was the same way in his community.

A third family was driving through the farmer's community and stopped to ask the same questions. The farmer asked them the same question as he asked the others, "How is the community where you come from?" The family stated that they love their community. Everybody got along and helped each other. They really hated the thought of having to leave their community. The farmer stated that it was the same way in his community.

You see, it is all about the attitude and perspective that you bring with you that determines your future experiences.

Chocolate covered peanuts:

I was lying in my rack one evening during the Desert Storm War. I really love chocolate covered peanuts. As I was lying there, I noticed that I had only four left. My last bag. As I was eating the first one, I was savoring it, and something distracted me. Crunch! I bit into it. Dang it! I put the second one in my mouth. Knowing that I wanted to keep it in my mouth, waiting for the candy shell to melt and reach the savory chocolate. "Hey Hope," somebody called out. Crunch! Dang it! I put the third one in my mouth. Patiently, savoring the taste. The candy shell was melting away, the savory chocolate thinning, I started to taste the film of the skin surrounding the peanut. Wham, I got hit in the arm. Crunch! Dang it. All I wanted to do was to savor those last chocolate covered peanuts until the end. Was that asking too much?

Then it hit me like a ton of bricks, as I reflected and compared the chocolate covered peanuts to life. We are not a cat with nine lives. We cannot just act as we wish, then ask for a do over, a mulligan, when things go wrong. We have but one life, and we must cherish each and every moment. Cherish it all.

You see, everything is all a matter of perspective and attitude.

I have struggled with PTSD for quite some time, whether I wanted to admit it or not. I can't believe what I put my family through. I can't believe the amount of patience they had with me, especially my lovely bride Christine. Again, I attest to you, there is "HOPE."

Before my PTSD therapy, I let myself get into an I- don't-care-about-anything attitude. An attitude I later learned is very typical of somebody needing therapy. I used to read all the time, I loved reading. During that PTSD time, I read nothing. I allowed myself to completely shut down. No reading, crafts, or other activities. I struggled with anxiety, increased arousal, avoidance, anger, irritability, guilt, shame, sadness, depression, and sexual impotency.

My therapy enabled me to become a new man. It enabled and empowered me to rekindle the appreciation for my great attitude on life. Yes, we can lose our attitude, or have a bad attitude, but we can also choose to find our good attitudes.

I also must give some recent credit to Andy Frisella, the founder of 75HARD and the 75HARD Challenge. The 75HARD Challenge consists of a commitment to 75 days straight with the following expectations:

- Follow a diet. Zero cheat meals for the entire 75 days.

- Workout 2X a day for at least 45-minutes. (One workout must be outside)

- Drink a gallon of water per day.

- Read 10 pages of a non-fiction entrepreneur book.

- Take a progress picture every day.

- No cheat meals or alcohol.

This challenge has enabled me to improve myself, by challenging me to become a better man. The reading of ten pages a day from a book that is entrepreneurial or self- improving has been awesome. Invigorating and opening the mind. It is amazing how just a little bit of concentrated effort can push you to the next level. My mental acuity has never been better.

Which is it going to be? Your choice - good or bad Attitude? What is your attitude toward life? Are you letting your childhood, your past, affect your future? "There is Hope."

So, what does this all mean, this ATTITUDE business?

Have you ever heard people say, "You can't always get what you want." In life, you often don't get what you want. But you do get what you expect. Or to put it another way, what you focus on is what you get. You've heard the expression, "Go looking for trouble and that's what you will find." It's true, and not only about trouble. It's true about everything. Go looking for conflict, and you will find it. Go looking for people to take advantage of you, and they generally will. See the world as a dog-eat-dog place, and you will always find a bigger dog looking at you as if you are his next meal. Go looking for the best people, and you will be amazed at how much talent, passion, ingenuity, empathy, and good you will find. Ultimately, the world treats you more or less the way you expect to be treated. In fact, you would be amazed at just how much you have to do with what happens to you.

Your Attitude is a Choice.

The average person waits for someone else to motivate them. They perceive that their circumstances are responsible for the way they think. But which comes first— the attitude or the circumstances? The truth is it doesn't matter which came first. No matter what happened to you yesterday, your attitude is your choice today.

Psychologist Victor Frankl believed, "The last of our human freedoms is to choose our attitude in any given circumstance." Frankl survived imprisonment in a Nazi death camp, and throughout his ordeal, he wouldn't allow his attitude to deteriorate. If he could maintain a good attitude, so can you.

Your Attitude Determines Your Actions.

Family expert Denis Waitley addressed this issue: "The winner's edge is not in a gifted birth, a high IQ, or in talent. The winner's edge is all in the attitude, not aptitude. Attitude is the criterion for success." Your attitude is crucial because it determines how you act and feel.

People are a Mirror of Your Attitude.

I am always amazed when people display a poor attitude but expect people around them to be upbeat. The law of magnetism really is true: who you are is who you attract.

Maintaining a good Attitude is Easier than Gaining One.

In the book Earth and Altar, Eugene H. Peterson wrote, "Pity is one of the noblest emotions available to human beings: self-pity is possibly the most ignoble… it is an incapacity, a crippling emotional disease that severely distorts our perception of reality… a narcotic that leaves its addicts wasted and derelict."

If you already have a positive attitude, I want to encourage you to keep it up. On the other hand, if you have a difficult time expecting the best of yourself and others, don't despair, because you can change your attitude.

Attitude is 10 percent what happens to you and 90 percent how you react to it. Be the change, make the difference! Attitude!

There is "HOPE."
God does give "HOPE."

CHAPTER 3

Assess, Adapt, Overcome

"Don't let challenges stump you,
provide the opportunity!"
—Blair D. Hope

You would expect one would learn assess, adapt, and overcome in the military. But, I had to learn this at a very young age.

One of my first childhood memories is a picture of me sitting on the gas meter in front of our duplex in Granger, UT. I was about four years old, holding a marijuana joint and a can of beer. That picture can really say a thousand words about my childhood. Let me be very clear. I love my family with all my heart, and I do not judge any of them for their actions or decisions they have made in their lives. Interestingly enough, I wish I could feel the same way when it comes to other's judgements against me. That is not a pity party statement, it was just my reality at that time. I share these stories as a matter of perspective, to show what I have experienced and overcome.

I'm sure many of us have had our own challenges in our own childhood and upbringing. Mine was no worse or better than some, it was just mine. My mother and father married young, my father was 18 and my mother was 16. They got married because my mother got pregnant at 15. As you can imagine, her family was not too happy with this, and treated her like the black sheep of the family. My mother's oldest sister was old enough to be my grandmother. Most of my mother's family stayed close to their religious beliefs, and they are good people. My father's family had more of a "c'est la vie" attitude toward life. Unfortunately, drugs, alcohol, crime, and divorce were traditional actions and behavior for them. I would estimate that 65 percent of my father's family have been in jail or prison.

My dad joined the Army shortly after getting married. My father went to boot camp in Fort Lewis, NC. His AIT training was at Fort Lee, VA. When he was stationed at Fort Lee, we lived in Hopewell, VA. I have photo memories of the historical battle sites of the Civil War. There were also photos of me as a toddler with bandages up to both elbows on my arms. My Father liked his coffee boiling hot and set a cup on the coffee table, where I grabbed it and spilled it all over my arms, receiving third degree burns on both arms. I still have scars today.

He was then stationed in Fort Bragg, NC, and he was shipped off to Bien Hoa, Vietnam. He was in supply, and was tasked with transporting the remains of deceased soldiers back to the states. He was also part of the death notification team (Casualty and Memorial Affairs Operations). Later, he was stationed at Fort McClellan, AL. My Father didn't like the Army. He got out of the Army because of his use of marijuana and going A.W.O.L.

My first memories of my father were when we lived in that duplex in Granger, UT. My father was a drunk and he loved his marijuana. We had a six-foot fence in our back yard, and the marijuana plants were just as tall as that fence. The leaves were the size of a man's hand. He loved the shape of the leaves and would dry some of them in the encyclopedia – they practically spanned the width of the whole page. Crazy! My Father loved Jimi Hendricks and other Woodstock bands. We had Jimi Hendrix and other psychedelic posters, and beads hanging in the doorways of our house.

My Father became very abusive to my mother. I remember one evening, it was very bad. The cops were called, and my dad ran away. I remember the cops coming and the red and blue lights in the darkness of the night. I was outside walking up and down the street. I remember seeing my father hiding behind a large green utility box down the street. Later that evening or early morning, he came back. When I got up in the morning and peered into my parents' bedroom, I saw my dad sleeping next to my mom. What kind of crazy crap is that! I remember my dad getting so mad at me one time, he kicked me so hard when I was on the floor, I flew into the hallway eight feet away. Why should any kid have to deal with that kind of atmosphere?

Well, obviously the marriage did not work and my dad left. My mother moved on and got a live in boyfriend, Steve. Steve was probably the closest thing I had to a real long-term Dad. A huge alcoholic, but he wasn't abusive and he cared for us kids. Shortly after Steve moved in, my dad was so pissed that he took a tire rim and threw it through the back window of Steve's car. Steve was a great guy, but his drinking and his relationship with my mother was not cohesive.

Steve loved hunting and spotting for deer and elk. One day, while spotting elk off I-80 up Parleys Canyon, in a pull-out viewing section, a semi-truck driver veered between his truck and the guard rail, hitting and killing Steve. That was really hard for me. Like I said, Steve was the closest thing I had to a long-term father. Steve and his family took us kids in like we were their own and loved us unconditionally. I called his sisters and brothers, aunts and uncles. I was often teased for telling people that I had so many aunts and uncles.

"God Gives Hope"

My father first went to prison for not paying child support, which was $180 a month for three kids. The other two times were for probation violations. I remember visiting my father in prison with my Grandma Hope. It seems everyone that goes to prison finds Jesus Christ, at least while they are incarcerated. My Father would write me letters, almost all of his letters included a message to stay close to Jesus Christ.

As a youth, I was always being invited to parties, to do drugs, and drink alcohol. Trust me, I wasn't an angel, but enough is enough. As a kid, I saw more drugs than most adults, briefcases of drugs. I knew I was meant for something better. I started making different decisions on activities and who I hung out with. My Family on the Hope side was beginning to treat me differently, like I was better than them for making different decisions. That's only half the problem. My Mother's family acted like they had a holier-than-thou attitude. They treated my mother like a black sheep. So how was I to make a decision that would distance myself from one family and not be accepted by the other family? Believe me, this really sucked. I felt so alone. My dad's family didn't want me because they thought that I was better than them. My mother's family didn't want me because I was not good enough. I felt alone for a very long time. When it comes to thinking about my families today, if I am being honest, I still feel lonely. I suppose that is one good reason I have learned to compartmentalize so well. I wish I was closer to all of my family, and we could accept each other for who we are.

There comes a time when one gains independence, thinks confidently, and acts confidently in their life, usually or hopefully around adulthood. My time came early in life, very early, probably around the age of 10 years old. Way too young for a child to become independent, act and care for himself. I later left the house as a young teenager.

My dad once told me, "Blair, you need to use me as an example." I exclaimed, "What!? Why would I use you as an example?" He said, "You need to use me as an example of what not to be in life, don't be like me." Wow!! What kind of father tells that to their kid? That takes a man with big balls. To one, admit to himself what kind of man he is. And two, to tell your own son, not to be like you, and tell him to be better than you. From that day on, I wanted to make my dad proud of me.

Having hardly any money growing up, with a single mom making minimal wages, it forced me to think outside the box and find ways to make money. I was very creative and persistent with people in convincing them to allow me to work for them.

I really had to:

Assess the situation...

I had to realize who my family was and their actions. I had to accept who they were. I had to recognize the reality of my situation. I had to realize who I was, where I was, and where I wanted to be.

Adapt to the situation...

I wanted to help myself. I had to adapt to the reality of the decisions I had made, to make different decisions, to improve my situation in life. Decisions that were far different than the way my family was living and the decisions that would take me on a much different path than my family.

Overcome the situation...

I had to overcome the reality of the outcome of my decisions. Man, was I not prepared for this outcome.

- Dad's family resented me because they thought I was better than them.
- Mom's family treated her like the black sheep and I felt she was not accepted, therefore I would not be accepted, because I was her son.

One of the hardest things in life is feeling like you have left your family behind. I felt horrible for leaving Blaine, my younger brother behind. I really love that kid. Years later, I found out how much he loved and missed me from a good friend of his before that friend died. Please don't wait until it's too late to mend things with those you love and care about, "HOPE,."

I later had to assess, adapt, and overcome my illiteracy and grammatic incorrectness. Realizing that you have a learning disability is not for the weak hearted. It's even harder when you want to get better and improve yourself. The embarrassment of being in resource classes. I used those ill feelings to drive me to improve and graduate from those resource classes.

In the Military you have to assess, adapt, and overcome as well. To a much different level.

We all have to overcome many things in life, large or small. It is all a matter of perspective on how we handle it. Assess, adapt, and overcome. I am here to tell you, that you don't have to be black, white, brown, yellow, or homosexual to feel alone. Anyone and everyone can feel very, very alone. Especially those that you think never would.

While in the Navy I was engaged to Jennie Reynolds, we were to be married February 14, 1991, Valentines Day. I was home bound from the Desert Strom Gulf War. I was so excited to get home and marry the girl I loved. I was supposed to be back from deployment early January of that year, and I did not get home until the end of April due to the war. Jennie sent me a dear John letter the later part of March and crushed my world. What do I do now?

Before deploying to the war, I had met a cute girl, Amy Kulwicki, at one of our young single adult activities. Great girl and fun to be with. Amy joined the Army and was stationed in Germany during the war. She was in an abusive relationship and had gotten pregnant and decided to get out of the Army. I received a letter from her on my way home explaining her situation and that she wanted to see me when I got home. I returned home and started seeing Amy and we were married in October 1991. I know I rushed the marriage, against the wishes of both sides of the families, especially my grandfather. We were only married three years and I was deployed for over half of the marriage.

After leaving the Navy and getting divorced from Amy, I went off grid for three months. I was a lost man trying to find my way. Finally landing my own apartment. I tried forcing several relationships to no avail. I started attending a single adult ward in our church. When the ecclesiastical leaders asked how long I would be with them, I said forever. Some young adult ladies finally talked me into going to a single adult dance.

I must admit I was getting excited about the opportunity. As fate would have it, the young ladies had to back out and would not be attending the dance. I decided to go alone. I arrived early and strategically positioned myself under the basketball standard in the church gym. And there I stayed – all night. I mean all night until the last two songs of the dance. I had been watching this gorgeous girl dance on the floor all night long. You must understand that I love dancing, and for me to stand under that basketball standard all night long like a wall flower, was unheard of. Before the second to last song started, that gorgeous blonde was standing not less than ten feet away. All of a sudden, I imagined myself walking towards Christine. Right then I decided to make it real and I went to her and asked Christine to dance. The song playing was Waterfalls, by TLC. Not exactly a slow or fast song, but we took the slow song position. We danced the second song. I asked Christine if she wanted to get a shake at a local restaurant. We did! We laughed and clicked right away. Somehow, I forgot my wallet and Christine had to pay for our shakes and fries. That was May 5th. We spent the weekend together and on Sunday morning, when Christine was putting shoes on the boys, I asked, what if I asked you to marry me what would you say? She said she would say yes. Well, she took that as a proposal, which was May 7th. I asked her father if I could have his daughter's hand in marriage and he approved. Her mother asked if I was doing the right thing, I said. It felt right. Her sister Serena knew, she went home the night of the singles dance and told her mother, "Christine met the man she is going to marry tonight." We were married July 22, 1995, less than three months after we met and have been married 28 years now. God does give Hope.

My world was rocked when I lost my hero, mentor, father figure, my mother's father Parley A. Sargent. I owe much gratitude to that man, taking me in unconditionally, teaching me accountability and responsibility. He passed away on April 18, 2004. I was still a young father and had much to learn. My grandfather was a very talented, independent, and stubborn man. But his heart was huge and full of love. He was everything to me and the closest thing I had to a father. I lived with him before I left for the U.S. Navy as well as when I got out of the U.S. Navy. He was there for me, believing in me, supporting me, and molding me.

It was so hard for me to see my grandfather in the nursing home, getting worse every day – and he didn't want to be there. The day before he passed, I was with him, affixing his adult diaper so that it would not fall off. My Hero, frail and breaking down. It hurt so bad. After helping him with his diaper, very solemnly, he stated to me, "Blair, I'm tired, I'm done, I want to be with Grandma," He passed early the next morning. My Aunt Joann called to inform me of his passing. It hit me like a ton of bricks.

I was emotionally crushed. I was asked to speak at his funeral, I spoke about him with pride and love, fitting for the hero that he was in my life. That day I had to choose not to give up. I believe I have lived my life so that he would be proud of me. Choosing not to give up is challenging. I tell you this because my own mother has not made the choice to "not give up." Even today, she deeply struggles with the loss of her mother and father and doesn't have a firm understanding of Heavenly Father's plan.

I have come to realize, that it gets harder because I am getting stronger. I don't run from the challenges, I accept them.

What is your situation? Have you accepted it? Have you assessed your situation? Have you identified and adapted to the changes you need? Have you overcome the hurdles in your way? Why not? Start now!

If you work hard, you own the finale.

There is "HOPE."
God does give "HOPE."

CHAPTER 4

Stay the Course

"Staying the course is key to winning any battle.
For victory, for honor. Are you willing to stay the course?"
—Blair D. Hope

It's interesting how we choose or don't choose to stay the course. When I was in high school, I enjoyed being with friends and dating girls. I met this girl, Blenda, and I was attracted to her in many ways. She wasn't only beautiful, but very outgoing and athletic. She kind of turned my world upside down with how I thought about her and what she taught me. My friends always teased me for saying: "This is the one." I was head over heels in love. Blenda played basketball, volleyball, and ran track.

I wanted to spend as much time as I could with her. But she was always playing or practicing a sport, so I decided to try out for the track team, maybe try the 400 relay. I was a cross country runner, so I figured the 400 relay shouldn't be that bad. When showing up for tryouts, Coach called out my name, "Hope, get over here." He wanted me to try out for the 100-meter and the 200- meter events. Crazy! I have never run sprints before. Although, I was known for running pretty fast in other sports.

They were about to have the 100 meter tryouts, and I joined in. I had never used starting blocks before, so I did not use one. The starting gun went off, I bolted, and I pulled my groin. But I still finished third in the trial. Crazy! Then I ran the 200 meter and placed first. Throughout the year, I qualified for the Junior Olympics to be held in Texas. Sweet! Well... there was one problem. Going from a cross country runner to a sprinter caused severe shin splints that led to stress fractures on both of my legs. After three electrode treatments, the doctor gave me a choice. I could continue to run, and break my legs, or I could quit. Ouch!! Give up on my goals? Or stay the course? Well, sometimes adversity leads to good things.

During my senior year at Taylorsville High School, while dating Blenda, I went to every single one of her sport events and the rest of the high school sport events. While attending a high school football game, I was making fun of the school mascot, "Wilber the Warrior." One thing led to another, and I got called to the counseling center. I was asked by a counselor, "I understand you would like to be Wilber the Warrior?"

Just like that, I was the school mascot, Wilber the Warrior. What a blast that was. All because I made the choice to better myself during my Senior Year.

Junior High – Wrestling

I always wanted to fit in. Be somebody. Do something great. In the seventh grade while attending Eisenhower Junior High School, I decided to wrestle. At 95 pounds I was just a little guy. Eighth grade, I wrestled at 105 lbs. Ninth grade, I wrestled at 115 lbs. I wanted the varsity spot so bad. To get it I had to wrestle Scott, THE best wrestler. Scott was a shorter guy but built like a brick house and strong as ever. Total athlete. I had to wrestle Scott for the number one slot on the team at 115 lbs. Yeah right!! It was a 30 to 1 odds that I would lose the match. I would likely be pinned in the first 30 seconds of the first round. I was determined not to go down that easy. If Scott was going to beat me, he was going to have to earn it. I was determined, he was NOT going to pin me. After the first round, no pin, I was still in the match. After the second round, no pin. After the third round no pin! I don't recall the exchange of points in each round. All I know is that I gave it my all for three solid rounds. Scott Wilberger did NOT pin me, and he only beat me by two points. I believe I earned Scott's respect that day.

I went into the locker room and cried. Yes, I cried. I was so emotional. I gave my best and I did not win. But the good part was that

I did not get pinned by one of the strongest and most popular kids in school. That was probably one of the biggest "wins" in my life. Yes, I said a win. I could have given up and folded under the pressure of being told I would lose the match, but I gave it my all. Awesome right? Not really. I gave up wrestling. Why? Because I thought I wasn't good enough. How could that be one of the best and worst feelings? I quit wrestling after that year. Scott later went on to be one hell of an athlete in wrestling, football, and baseball. He is now a decorated police officer in a K-9 unit protecting our local freedoms. God bless him.

MORE Wrestling

During my Junior year in high school, my mother made us move to Ontario, Oregon with her boyfriend, Dale, a truck driver. What a prick he was. I will talk about him later.

While attending Ontario High School for one semester, I met a good friend Bill. Bill was a great baseball player and wrestler. He talked me into trying out for the wrestling team. I made the team and lost a match to a kid from Weiser, Idaho. Those farm boys are strong. In a suicide cradle move (which he executed perfectly) he pinned me. Once again, I gave up and quit. Why? Because once again I thought I was not good enough.

Now for Dale. He was the reason I left home at such an early age. Dale was a very abusive man. He was abusive to my mom and my sister. I had no tolerance for abusiveness, due to my real father. My mother made me promise that I would not do anything to cause a scene and ruin her life. I reluctantly agreed.

There is not much to do in Ontario, Oregon, except to work and go to school. So that is what I did. I worked at an ice cream place and a local restaurant as a cook. I saved all my money and placed it into my very first bank account. I had a lot of money saved and often gave my mother money for what she needed. I bought the very TV I was watching when Dale came into the living room drunk. It was a Saturday morning, and I was watching TV in the living room while lying on the couch in my bathrobe. I worked hard and was just chilling out on my day off.

Dale walked in, very drunk, and started cussing at me, stating that I was a "lazy son of a bitch," and so on. I ignored him, and he continued. He threw his tumbler of alcohol at the TV and broke it, shattering the glass tumbler as well. By now I had enough. I stood up, and he said, "What are you going to do?" "I'm not going to do anything," I stated. He said, "I am going to kick your ass."

He took one swing and missed, then he swung again and landed a punch on my shoulder. I had to defend myself, and I defeated him. I got dressed and left the house.

I walked directly to the bus station. I got to the counter to purchase a one-way ticket back to Salt Lake City. I then realized I left in such a hurry, I forgot my checkbook, so I had no money. I walked around town all day and into the evening trying to figure out what to do. I ran into my friend Bill, and he was kind of freaked out. He told me that the cops came by his house six different times looking for me. I decided that if the cops were looking for me, I would walk to the police station and turn myself in. I walked into the police station and said, "My name is Blair Hope, apparently you are looking for me." She told me to wait and walked to a back room. Out walked this huge police officer, tall and muscular, he was a sergeant.

He asked, "Are you Blair Hope?" "Yes sir," I stated. "Please come with me." He led me to the back interview room. As we entered he grabbed my shoulder and placed himself between my mother, Dale, and myself. Dale stood up as he saw me enter the room. The sergeant placed his right hand on Dale and firmly pressed Dale back in his seat, with his bandages and injuries.

We sat down at the table and the sergeant asked, "Are you ok?" I told him yes. He asked me to tell him what happened that morning and where I was all day. I told him everything. I had done nothing wrong in my eyes. After hearing my story, the sergeant, looked at my mother and said, "Mrs. Hope, it appears you need to make a choice here. Your son, or this…" as he waved his hand at Dale. My mother, started to cry and said, "Don't make me make a choice."

Well, as the result of her choice, I was sent to a foster home until further notice. The foster home was pretty cool. The family had a fairly large home, plenty of room for foster kids. The family raised Greyhound racing dogs. They had a racetrack and everything. I got to feed the dogs and watch them chase a fake rabbit racing down a rail along the track. It was fascinating. Then came the day when I was able to go to my grandfather in Utah.

Believe it or not, somehow my mother talked Dale into giving me a ride back to Salt Lake City. Awkward! Not a word was said between Dale and I during the whole trip. He dropped me off at a truck stop in Salt Lake City where my grandfather picked me up. That was the summer before my senior year in high school.

Back to Utah - alone

I started my senior year back at Taylorsville High School. I just wanted a positive change in my life. Lots of great things happened during that year. I lived with my best friend Chris Miller and then with my grandfather, Parley Sargent. I will be forever indebted to Chris Miller, his mother, Barbara Miller, Andy Jackson, and his mother, Myrna Jackson. Barbara Miller let me live with her family when I had no place to go. Barbara and Myrna made sure that I was treated with love, and they provided for my needs. They provided me with love and even Christmas gifts, taking from their own families. The unconditional love I received from their families is priceless. I will never forget them. God Bless them.

I only took one year of LDS Seminary and that was during my Senior year. The Church of Jesus Christ of Latter-day Saints provides seminary classes for high school kids. The schools provide release time from school so kids can go to the seminary building, take a class and return. One of the awesome experiences I had during seminary during my senior year was that I was placed in a class full of juniors. I was the only senior. As a testament to the desire to change my life my senior year, all the juniors elected me to be their class president. Nothing special really, just a confirmation that I was being looked after, and looked up to. My seminary teacher ended up being a mentor and good friend of mine for life.

Helicopter Crash

The things we go through and experience in life can make or break us if we allow them too. While in the Navy, one of the traumatic incidents I encountered really bothered me. It bothered me longer than I could ever imagine.

On October 8, 1990, at approximately 0415 two UH- 1N helicopters from the HMM squadron, launched from the U.S.S. Okinawa LPH-3 for an "at sea NVG (Night Vision Goggles) training operation" off the coast of Oman (North Arabian Sea). At 0513 the two helicopters disappeared from radar and failed to respond to radio calls. Observers on the flight deck saw a ball of fire dropping into the sea. Search efforts recovered very little wreckage and no sign of the aircrew. All were declared missing at sea. The eight men aboard were considered the first casualties of Operation Desert Shield. This training OP and many others were work ups to the missions we were planning during the Gulf War.

Those men were great men, all of them. We trained hard for those missions. Trained to perfection, anything can go wrong. This tragic accident has stuck with me for over 30 years.

I mention this story in this chapter of "Stay the Course" for two reasons. One: The loss of eight great men, eight men that I worked with, trained with, ate with, laughed with. To lose them instantly, gone! I couldn't tell their families and loved ones of their loss. It was hard to view eight empty caskets in the hangar, draped with the American flag. How was I to accept that? How could I possibly move on? How do I compartmentalize that? To move on, I had to make a decision to stay the course.

Two: Later on in life, thirty years later, that awesome compartmentalization began to fail and implode. I had to seek help and therapy and once again, I was forced to make a decision to "Stay the Course." I had to make conscious mental decisions to be healthy, to save my marriage and keep my family together. Are you willing to make the decisions to "Stay the Course"?

Working for Proctor & Gamble has been such a blessing in my life. When I was told that I would not be considered for promotion because of my English and grammar scores on my assessment test, did I give up? No! I stayed the course. I found out there was a way forward despite the perceived rule. The result of my determination? I was presented with a written offer, "The Golden Key" and I accepted. I was now on an equal playing field with my other counterparts in the company.

They also said a master's degree was required. I did not allow the fact that I did not have a master's degree stop me. Let alone a bachelor's degree or even an associate's degree. I stayed the course. I am now a senior executive with P&G.

How many of us get bogged down with the mundane day to day routine, the excuses that we let distract us? How many of us focus on the details of so many little things that we lose focus of the larger picture?

Are you willing to be the one person to stand up, speak the truth, when it is not popular and go against the masses?

There is "HOPE."
God does give "HOPE."

CHAPTER 5

Marketing and Exposure

"It's my job to make you look good,
and by default I look good."
—Blair D. Hope

Two of my favorite words are, "marketing" and "exposure." Everything we do in life, in our careers, in our communities, within our families, everything we do is somehow related to marketing and exposure.

Have you ever heard somebody say, "I could never be a salesman?" I say to them: "You better be a salesman, and a damn good one!" Every single day we are selling who we are, our personalities, our talents, traits, and passions. Think of it as self-promotion. Building our credibility. If we are NOT selling, or marketing ourselves on a daily basis, what does that say for our life's desires, ambitions or initiatives?

Are you in the right place? How well do you want to provide for your family? Do you want your family to believe in you? Do you want a better life? Do you want to progress in your career? Then you better be marketing and promoting yourself. You better be marketing yourself to the same level or better than you want out of life. Don't sell yourself short. That includes taking a job or getting into a career because somebody else wants you to do that.

I don't care how smart you are, what your G.P.A. was in school, what or how many degrees you have. If you are not willing or able to present yourself and apply the knowledge you have learned in an attractive and contagious way, you are selling yourself short.

I heard a story of a father who continually told his son, get this electronic engineering degree and you are guaranteed $90,000 a year. I laughed. Not being rude, but nothing is guaranteed. The son graduated with that degree and became a rocket scientist, not making $90,000. Now I am not saying he did anything wrong, and he still landed a great salary, but it was not a guarantee. He realized it was not the job for him. He didn't like being stuck in a cubical every day. He wanted something more out of life, something where he could feel he was making a difference. He left that job, studied for the MCAT exam, and practically aced it. He later became an eye surgeon, and now has his own practice, a very nice home, but most importantly he has a beautiful family. I can tell you, that man learned to assert himself, present his qualities, and apply his talents and knowledge. He learned to "market" himself to society.

All throughout my life and career I have used marketing and exposure to benefit the different projects, causes, and programs I have been involved in. More importantly, I found ways to enable and empower others to believe in themselves, and realize the importance of showing up to present and market whatever cause they are involved in.

Marketing: a) the act or process of selling or promoting in a market. b) the process or technique of promoting, selling, and distributing a product or service.

Exposure: the condition of being exposed: such as a: being presented to view or made known; b: being subject to some effect or influence.

Whatever career you are in, whatever club, program, cause, or campaign you get behind, there is always or should be an objective and mission statement. The question is, how are you going to let people know about your objectives or mission statements? This goes the same for you as a person. How do you go about marketing yourself and letting others know of your objectives and what you are all about?

So how do you market yourself? To begin, you have to show up!

The way you present your objectives must be clear, concise, but most importantly, it has to be attractive and contagious. If your audience cannot feel your excitement and see the vision you are trying to portray, then you will not gain their attention or support. But that cannot even begin to happen unless you show up.

Share of Mind or Mindshare

Years ago, I came upon a saying, "Share of Mind."

Others may refer to it as Mindshare.

Mindshare or Share of Mind definition: an approach to marketing that involves making a company, brand or product, or a person (YOU) the first one that comes to mind when a customer thinks of a particular market or topic.

Some ways to achieve this could include a catchy jingle, careful positioning, strong social media presence and calculated communication by marketing teams.

The greatest success of Mindshare takes place when a company's name or product name becomes interchangeable in common vernacular with the product itself, also known as top of mind. Examples of this include Q-tip, Xerox, Kleenex, and Hoover.

I took this definition and made it a bit more personal, applying it to people and a team objective. "How often do you or they think of me and my objective, when I am not there?" Reflect on that for a minute – other people thinking of you, or your objective, when you are not there.

In my world as a regional sales manager for Procter & Gamble, as well as being a leader in the Boy Scouts of America, more specifically, The Order of the Arrow program as Lodge Advisor, it has been imperative that I apply "Share of Mind" to enable and empower, both professional and volunteer teams to work towards their own, or my, objectives.

So how do you do that? Know your objectives. Are you passionate about them? Do you believe in them? Take a personal interest in those on your team. Do they know you're sincere? Does your team understand the importance and urgency behind the mission of your objectives? Do they know how those objectives can improve their lives? Do they know how meeting those objectives improves their team or their community?

It's my job to make you look good...

To enable this "Share of Mind" philosophy, I came up with a saying, that I have put into action.

"It is my job to make you look good, and by default I look good."

Reflect on that for a moment… It's your job to make them look good, by default you look good. As a leader, everything good and bad rolls up to you. It behooves you to do everything you can to make your team look good, then by default you look good.

I found this to be true. I made a point to train them on the knowledge, the product, or the objective, with all the features and benefits. I taught them to present the way I would present with their own personal touch. I helped them with their first sales calls, closing sales for them and giving them the credit. I believed in them and inquired about their families. To this day, they know I sincerely care about them.

That same saying, "It is my job to make you look good, and by default I look good," works for your upper management as well. Who do you report to? Who is your leader? Are you clear on their objective? Are they clear on your objective? It is your job to make your manager look good, by default you look good. If you make sure your manager looks good, it will make life much easier for you to meet your objectives and build more resources. The future of your career just started looking much better.

How? Why? Because you just created "Share of Mind" when you made your manager look good. That manager now automatically thinks of you FIRST before anyone else, even when you are not present.

Share of Mind Principles

"Whatever you are, be a good one."—Abraham Lincoln

Principle 1: Everyone makes a Difference.

It doesn't matter how large or how ineffective an organization is, an individual can still make a difference. A mediocre employer or leader can hinder exceptional performance, choose to ignore it, and not adequately recognize or encourage it. An excellent employer or leader can enable employees to achieve exceptional performance and then reward it. Ultimately, only the employee or volunteer can choose to do his or her job in an extraordinary way, regardless of the circumstances.

Reflect on it. Do you add to or take away from the experience of your customers, teams, or colleagues? Do you move your organization closer to or further from its goals? Do you perform your work in an ordinary way, or do you execute with excellence? Do you lighten someone's burdens or add to it? Do you lift someone up or put someone down?

Nobody can prevent you from choosing to be exceptional. At the end of the day, the only questions that matter are: What kind of difference do you want to make? What do you want your legacy to look like?

Martin Luther King Jr. said: *"If a man is called to be a street sweeper, he should sweep streets even as Michelangelo painted or Beethoven composed music or Shakespeare wrote poetry. He should sweep streets so well that all the hosts of heaven and earth will pause to say, 'Here lived a great street sweeper who did his job well.'"*

Setting a higher standard is more challenging than simply achieving the status quo. Withstanding the criticism of those who are threatened by your achievement depends not on your title, but on your attitude. The more valuable you are to others, the more value you create in your work or your interactions with others, the more value will eventually flow toward you – the more "Share of Mind." Faithfully doing your best, independent of the support, acknowledgment, or reward of others, is a key determinant in a fulfilling career.

Principle 2: Success is built on Relationships.

I believe success in sales is 80 percent relationships and 20 percent product or objective. I feel the biggest reason for my success in selling for Procter & Gamble is my relationships I have made with my distributors and customers.

It's easy to see why some stand above the crowd. Indifferent people deliver impersonal service. Service becomes personalized when a relationship exists between the provider and the customer. A successful salesperson takes time to get to know people and understand their needs and preferences. They then use that information to provide a better service than they ever received before. Do you have this capability?

Market share is proof that in any job or business, relationship building is the most important objective because the quality of the relationship determines the quality of the product or service.

Principle 3: Continually create value for others.

Do you ever complain that you don't have enough money? Do you lack the necessary training? Do you have the right opportunities? In other words, do you believe that you lack resources to perform at a higher level?

You must master the most important skill in the twenty-first century, the ability to create value for customers without spending more money to do it. You can replace money with imagination. The object is to outthink your competition rather than outspend them.

Are you concerned about being a victim of downsizing, and losing your job? Have you ever thought about changing your frame of mind from being employed, to being employable? When managing my team with Procter & Gamble, I have coined a phrase, "promotion worthy." Have you made yourself promotion worthy? Do you look for ways to add value to yourself? Do you look for opportunities to cross-train yourself? Do you add value to your team?

In today's economy, a high school or college graduate should expect to be unemployed a few times during his career. But that unemployment will be brief if he is employable – added value. Being employable means having a skill set that makes you desirable to any employer (i.e., promotion worthy, regardless of industry).

So what does that skill set and being "promotion worthy" look like? Many factors contribute to employability, but I submit to you that the most critical skill is the ability to create value for your customers and colleagues. Added value created for them is added value created for the team and the objective.

Principle 4: Reinvent yourself regularly.

Here is something to reflect on: If it is your job to make somebody else look good, by default you look good, how much could you and I do to bring originality to what we do? How can we reinvent ourselves and our work?

There are days when you wake up tired. You have read the books, listened to the podcasts, watched the videos, and completed the trainings. You are doing everything you can to produce personal excellence, but you are still tired and unmotivated. When your life is at low tide, when your professional commitment is wavering and you just want to get the job done and go home at the end of the day, what can you do?

I think of the people who have given service to me. Because if that person can bring that kind of creativity and commitment to serving others, I can do as much or more to reinvent my work and rejuvenate my efforts. I believe that no matter what job you have, no matter what industry you are in, or where you live, every morning you wake with a clean slate. You can make your business, as well as your life, anything you choose it to be. "Choose to wake up happy."

"There comes a special moment in everyone's life, a moment for which that person was born. That a special opportunity, when he seizes it, will fulfill his mission – a mission for which he is uniquely qualified. In that moment, he finds greatness. It is his finest hour." —Winston Churchill

Making a Difference

"The person doing the work determines the difference between mundane and magnificent." —Mark Sanborn

Your Choice

Which do you prefer, happiness or misery? Feeling good about your work or feeling bad about your work? Being yourself or hiding the real you? Is it harder to be negative, miserable, and insincere than it is to be happy, positive, and genuine? Choose to make those characteristic changes, no matter what type of work you do.

Most people think they get ahead in life by learning something new. I believe they also get ahead by going back to the basics of success. There are lots of ways to define success, but I believe that having the most fun doing your best work in serving people is at the top of the list. My grandfather, Parley A. Sargent told me that the definition of success is defined as, "The number of people at your bedside at your death."

Do the right thing for the right reason.

If you only expect praise and recognition, it will seldom come. Life has demonstrated that if your motive for doing something is to receive thanks or praise, you will often be disappointed. However, if you go about doing the right thing, knowing that doing the thing is its own reward, you will be fulfilled whether you get recognition from others or not. When reward or recognition comes, it will be icing on the cake.

"The reward of a job well done, is to have done it." —James Timberlake

There is "HOPE."
God does give "HOPE."

CHAPTER 6

Persistency and Consistency

"There's no such thing as luck."
—Blair Hope

Persistency and consistency will always win!

Timing is everything. At any given time, you have to place yourself in a position to be ready to take advantage of any opportunity that presents itself, right in front of you without warning.

Have you prepared yourself to be ready when the opportunity arises? Have you persued your goals and announced yourself to take the challenge or position when it confronts you? Are you taking advantage of the blessings and opportunities that cross your path?

I learned and applied a saying in my life, "promotion worthy." It should be your goal to be promotion worthy at any given time. Not that you will be promoted anytime soon, or should expect to be promoted soon. But are you the one they will consider when that promotion comes along?

I took advantage of many opportunities that came before me. When I was in the Navy, my peers thought I was crazy to go after the qualification program of the Aviation Warfare Specialist (AW Wings). They told me I was too young, not experienced enough, and many other negativities. All of this pessimism actually drove me harder to prove all of them wrong.

I studied hard. I had to learn all aspects of aviation warfare. The qualification process to obtain this insignia begins with the Enlisted Aviation Personal Qualification Standards, also known as PQS. There are two PQS for the Enlisted Aviation Warfare Specialist insignia. The first is the Common Core which consists of concepts, policies, and tasks that are common throughout Naval aviation and provide a foundation for a sailor's knowledge. The second is a platform-specific PQS which consists of several training tasks and other practical experience on-the-job exercises relevant to the particular aviation in the community the sailor is currently serving in, for example the HMM-164 squadron and the amphibious warfare carriers. The entire Enlisted Aviation PQS normally takes approximately one year to complete from the point of entering the enlisted aviation community, though it can be completed much earlier with a high degree of dedication and effort. I completed my qualification in less than six months.

Those completing the Enlisted Aviation PQS must then pass a written examination and a review board conducted by senior enlisted aviation personnel. Upon passing both the examination and the oral board, the Enlisted Aviation Warfare Specialist insignia is presented. The sailor is then authorized to add the Enlisted Aviation Warfare designator (AW) after his rate.

I later took advantage of an opportunity put before me when I was working for the pager company as well as other employers. I became great friends with an owner of a wireless distributor I was managing. His company seemed to be expanding rapidly. In passing I mentioned that the small community I lived in could benefit from his business locating there. He offered me my own location in Tooele, UT. I informed him that there was no way I could personally fund the start-up cost of a retail location. He offered to fund the operation and gave me a contract stating that I would pay him back in six months. I paid him back within three months. That company literally saved our house.

Another great opportunity showed up just when I needed it most. When I lost my job with a telecommunication company, as the corporate account manager, I was also working for a merchandising company. When

I lost my job, my wife was pregnant with our youngest son, Bridger. I needed benefits right away.

I had invested a great deal of time and effort to network with people in various businesses I associated with. This paid off big time because within a few hours of losing my job, I had three job offers with full benefits. I called my dotted line boss with P&G and informed him that I lost my fulltime job and that I have three job offers on the table. Spice told me to give him at least a couple of weeks before he would make a decision. I told him that I was letting him know right then and there.

He was able to meet with my manager Matt who worked with me at a previous telecommunications company. Matt stepped up and offered more hours for me, so I could provide for my family. He gave me 39 hours a week, part time back then. Then Spicer went out of his way to get me hired with P&G. The hiring process with P&G was typically a sixth month process. Spice got it done faster. I received an official offer letter in less than two months.

"God does give Hope."

When I got hired with P&G, it was not the salary that was discussed, it was $17,000 less than I was currently earning. But I did not give up.

I was told that I wasn't going to be promoted because of my assessment scores in English and grammar. Bummer. I did not give up.

National HR Manager – Golden Key

I was at a national sales meeting shortly after being hired at P&G. I happened to be speaking with the national H.R. manager. I mentioned that I had been told that I was unable to be promoted because of my assessment scores in English and grammar. You should have seen his face. "Who told you that?" he asked. "It doesn't matter, I just want to know if it is true," I said. He said it was not true and that if my manager wanted to get with him to discuss the issue, he would welcome the conversation.

He stated that, "when you receive the official job offer and get hired with P&G, you receive the "Golden Key." You are equal to others and you are on the same playing field.

I can tell you that I have "stayed the course." I have tried to be the best I can be. I have been promoted twice. I have been blessed financially, largely due to the fact that I decided to "stay the course." Persistency and consistency will always prevail.

What if I had told Matt, "No I am not interested in your offer," the offer that has led to my 20 plus year career with P&G?

What if YOU say no to an opportunity?

Sometimes persistency and consistency can be distracting and misleading. When I was a salesman for the pager company, a good friend of mine, Martin, owned a franchise of an investment company. He was beta testing a new recruitment tool in the form of an aptitude test in the personal finance industry. He had me take the exam as a favor to him. I passed the test with flying colors, and he wanted to hire me because I was a perfect fit for that industry.

I have to admit, the sound of that was intriguing. The status of being a financial planner for others - yeah right. Who was I to believe that? I was only about 27 years old, what financial advice could I give anybody? Martin was an established older gentleman with experience. You could tell why people would listen to him, he looked like he knew what he was talking about. He had more acronyms at the end of his title than any man I knew. Christine and I were renting a house and living paycheck to paycheck. I was going to school, working full time and delivering pizza part time for extra money. No financial advice could be offered by me, except survival.

Then I met a guy, Max, closer to my age, who really intrigued me. He introduced me to the owner of a financial planning company. Turns out Max and I knew of each other because we were both leaders in the Boy Scout program. He said he respected my work ethics and offered me a job on the spot, my own office, cherry wood credenza and everything. Now if that doesn't excite a self-inspiring man. All I had to do was pass the Series 6 financial exam and the job was mine.

I took all the practice exams I could. I was acing all of them and was feeling very confident about taking the actual exam. When ready, I scheduled my Series 6 exam at the testing center. I felt really good while taking the exam. I finished the exam, got my results, and I missed passing by three questions. I couldn't believe it, I was devastated.

Oh well, I decided to go back, study, and take the exam again. I took more practice exams, acing them all. I scheduled the second exam, paid another $85, and missed passing the exam by three questions. I couldn't believe it. This was for sure the career path for me, why did I not pass this exam? I was determined. I studied more and took more practice exams, and aced them all. I scheduled the third exam, paid another $85, and missed passing the exam by three questions.

After they scored my last exam, they informed me that they had given me the series 7 exam in error. This was the tougher qualification, and I only missed it by three questions. What in the world? Imagine if I had been so persistent in passing that exam?

Christine and I were meeting with our real estate agent, Marina, later that same day. We were about to close on our first new, custom built home. We put a lot of sweat equity into that home and were very excited to start this new chapter in our lives. Marina asked me if I was okay, and noted that I was not my typical happy energetic self. I told her about not passing the exams, and how bummed I was for not being able to start a new career. She looked sincere but perplexed, and then stated, "It's a good thing you didn't pass that exam and take that new job." I remarked, "What? How could you say that?"

"Blair, you need to understand, that if you were to quit your job in the telecommunications industry and take the job in the financial industry, you would lose your home. If you can't show employment for at least six months in a new industry, they will not loan you money for your new home," she explained. Wow! The Lord was really looking out for me. "God Does Give Hope."

This reminds me of another story where the Lord truly does look after me. Earlier on, while working for the pager company, I was always trying to better my financial situation to provide for my family. My friend Troy, introduced me to his wife Rene who worked for a communications company. She stated that they were looking for good candidates to sell communication systems, business phone systems, voice over IP, video, and so on. She said it wouldn't hurt having a conversation with the general manager to explore new options.

While discussing the job opportunity with the GM, he asked what it would take to get me to join his team. For the first time I felt confident to name my price, not knowing the outcome, I said $40,000 salary plus commissions. Done, he said. Welcome to the team. Okay, now what? I was still employed by the pager company. I informed him that I would have to give notice to my current employer first. "No problem," he said.

I tendered my notice right away. The manager was extremely sad to see me go and did everything he could to get me to stay. He was also excited to see that I wanted to improve myself and broaden my horizons.

I started the job with the communications company. Just when I was getting a good understating and knowledge of the products in the industry, a week later, the GM pulled everybody into the conference room. I remember saying, "Here we go, we are all on the chopping block." When we were all gathered in the room, apparently the GM overheard my statement, and said "Well, Blair is correct, the corporate office in Texas has decide to close the doors on the Utah office." Well that was it, I was unemployed. Devastated, but confident in a weird way, I had the day off.

Not sure what to do, I went to watch the High School Baseball State Championship games. I was a high school umpire back then and always enjoyed watching the championship games, before I took the field to umpire my game. While arriving at the field, I decided to call my old GM at the pager company. If you recall, he did not want me to leave the company and wanted me to stay. I called him at his office, "Hey, how are you? Are you sitting down," I asked. "Yes, why?" He asked. "Can I have my job back?"

"Sure, but your open sales job has been filled, all I have available is the resell manager position open." I quickly said: "That's not out of the question, I will take that position if that's okay with you."

"Great, see you Monday," he replied. I thanked him, and then called my wife Christine, and told her the story. I wasn't unemployed for long, was I?

"God Gives Hope" – Do you trust him?

Are you persistent and consistent? Do you make sure you are promotion worthy? Do you place yourself in positions so that when the time comes, you are ready to react? Are your network and intimate connections unified to better yourself among men?

Do you have a plan to be persistent and consistent to meet your dreams and goals? What are they? Have you written them down?

There is "HOPE."
God does give "HOPE."

CHAPTER 7

Do You Have What It Takes?

"Don't do your best, do whatever it takes."
—Blair D. Hope

Have you ever felt like you were David, in the David and Goliath story? Have you ever felt that you were just not good enough? Even though you knew you were better than the guy next to you, but you just didn't have the strength or attitude to take the next step.

What does it take? Luck?

- I don't believe in luck. It's all about timing.
- Practice the operation, sales pitch, product knowledge, mastery of skills.
- If you are prepared and have positioned yourself, when the time comes you will be ready to execute.

When I joined the Navy, I wanted to do well and excel at everything, and do something with my life. I wanted to make the Navy my career and retire in the Navy. I really didn't have any goals in life. But my biggest hurdle was, I still didn't think I was good enough.

So, my plan at the time was to take what was placed before me and make the best of it. Bad plan really, in retrospect. I'm glad something excited me about rank advancement and special training. Before I first enlisted in the Navy, I obtained the rank of Eagle Scout in the Boy Scouts of America. By earning the rank of Eagle Scout, it awarded me an automatic rank advancement to E-3 in the Navy, which enabled me to progress faster.

I was the youngest man in my command to achieve the rank of Petty Officer 3rd Class, E-4. I was also the youngest man in the command, both in rank and age, to earn my Aviation Warfare Specialist wings (AW). I remember the qualifications for this. It was meant to take you out of your comfort zone. You had to be more than familiar with aviation warfare tactics, flight tactics and more (as mentioned in Chapter 6).

For some reason, I had become lazy and complacent with further rank advancements. I really didn't care. Again, my evil demon of "I am not good enough" and I didn't deserve another rank advancement attitude. Of course, it didn't help at the time that President Clinton had frozen all rank advancement in the Navy.

Do you have what it takes?

That is a serious question a man must ask himself. One - Does he dare ask himself that question? Or is he just a follower and a sheep? Two - Does he have what it takes and take action to change the course of his life, family, or career? This had become a very serious problem for me.

One of the most pivotal points in my life is when I was invited to attend a Christian retreat hosted by a men's ministry called, Marked Men for Christ (MMFC). I was invited by my manager at the time who was the co-founder of MMFC, Steve "Spice" Spicer. That weekend literally changed my life.

I owe my life to Jesus Christ, but I owe a challenged spiritual journey to become closer to Jesus Christ to "Spice." I also owe my career of 20 plus years with P&G to "Spice" as well. He was my boss, my mentor, my friend, and my brother.

The MMFC weekend, it offers an intense, masculine, God honoring, non-judgmental, safe, and Holy Spirit driven atmosphere. I encourage all men to attend the powerful hard core 44-hour soul searching weekend. Why should you attend this 44-hour experience?

1. You will be challenged.

2. You will be encouraged.

3. You will grow and mature in your faith.

4. You will find connections with other men.

Is it for you? It is! Be the man God created you to be.

> Anger – is your anger serving you well?
> Fear – is fear paralyzing your life?
> Shame – is shame running your life?
> Loss – Are you experiencing Loss and depression?

"Spice" wrote a book called "Be Strong! The making of a Marked Man." I highly recommend this book. In his book, he talks about the wounds that hold us men back from properly healing and, becoming better men, and strengthening our relationship with Jesus Christ.

> Deceit: What mask do you wear? Fear: What are you afraid of?
> Anger: Get out of my way.
> Sadness: Grieving the loss of hopes, dreams, and relationships
> Forgiveness: Giving and receiving forgiveness.

"Be Strong! I'm in!"

If you are a man, desiring to be a better man, husband, father, brother, through healing and serving others, you might want to check out the Marked Men for Christ.

MY MISSION STATEMENT: "As a marked man for Christ, a husband, father, grandfather, and brother, I co- create a world of courage and honor, I do this through leadership, wisdom, and being like Peter the Rock."

The question we must ask ourselves is this, "When you recall what others have heaped upon you, is that memory still an open wound, a scab, or is it a healed fading scar?"

There was another major pivotal point in my life. For twenty years my wife Christine had been trying to get me to seek help with my Post Traumatic Stress Syndrome (PTSD).

PTSD can develop after a very stressful, frightening or distressing event, or after a prolonged traumatic experience.

Types of events that can lead to PTSD include:

- serious accidents
- physical or sexual assault
- abuse, including childhood or domestic abuse
- exposure to traumatic events at work, including remote exposure
- serious health problems, such as being admitted to intensive care
- childbirth experiences, such as losing a baby
- the death of someone close to you
- war and conflict
- torture

PTSD develops in about 1 in 3 people who experience severe trauma. If you are experiencing PTSD from any cause, hopefully my experience will motivate you to get help.

First, I had to admit that I had a problem. Second, I had to seek help. Third, I had to accept the help and acknowledge the impact it was having on my life. And fourth, I had to apply what I had learned and take action to make changes in my life.

I had tried once before with our family doctor. I went with my wife to an appointment and spilled my guts to the doctor, well at least what I wanted him to know. He was overwhelmed with all my issues and stated that he did not have time to help me. As you can imagine, this did not bode well with my psyche and drove me further into compartmentalization and deepened the PTSD.

I had a problem. I will never forget the day when I caught myself standing on the stairs up to my office at home, yelling at my kids at the top of my lungs. For what? I cannot tell you because I don't remember. It scared the hell out of me. Right then and there, I had an epiphany. I decided it was time to get help. I was asked many times by doctors and therapists, why now? After 25 years, why seek help. I would continually tell them, I'm sure I could give you plenty of excuses, but here is the only one that matters....

When the pain became so intense it became more powerful than my ego. When I reached that point I knew I needed to get help.

I had promised myself, and more importantly my wife Christine, that if I agreed to seek help, that I would lay it all out, everything. I would not hold back anything from the doctors. I would be an open book.

I must tell you, I was forewarned by many of my veteran brothers, that it could take up to 6 to 8 months to get an appointment with a primary care doctor at the VA. My decision was made, I told everyone, "I'm in. I will take whatever comes my way, whatever the time frame. I must get help."

After I received my VA identification card, I walked over to the Primary Care Clinic to make an appointment with my new doctor. I walked up to the appointment desk in the clinic and requested to make an appointment. The girl behind the desk looked at me with a little reservation, knowing it would take 6 to 8 months to get an appointment. She looked at the schedule, looked back at me and asked, "Are you somebody special?" I laughed, and said, "Not really, special K maybe." Then she asked, "Well, we just had a cancellation, how does this Thursday work for you?" I was in the right place at the right time. Timing is everything. "I'm in!"

I made my appointment with my new doctor in the Primary Care Department, Blue Clinic. The George E Whalen Veterans Hospital was also a training hospital, partnering with a neighboring medical school within the University of Utah. I mention this because one of my pet peeves is repeating myself to others when it comes to my personal issues, because I did not want to be there in the first place, I didn't want to admit I had issues, and something was wrong. Telling my story over and over again was not something I wanted to do.

They called my name and escorted me into the exam room, and I was told the doctor would be in shortly. Things just got real! It was time to be honest, transparent, and candid. In walked a young, good-looking, female resident doctor, an intern just out of medical school. I knew I was going to have to explain myself twice. Crap!

Well, here we go. I mentioned that I was not going to hold anything back. So, I dumped everything on her as to why I was there. All of it, the depression, emotions, stress, combat, the helicopter accident, the deaths, and carnage. I got emotional. She got so emotional that she began to cry. I left nothing out. I told her everything that I was dealing with. She composed herself, then excused herself and stated that the doctor would be in shortly.

Now, as I stated, the intern was a young good-looking woman, then the "real" doctor walked in. Wow! This doctor was knock out gorgeous. I say this because here I am waiting to unveil all my weaknesses and open my heart in a manly way. I am not expecting to do this with a gorgeous woman, I suppose I was expecting a burly man with an attitude of buck up and deal with it.

I retold all the stories, feelings, and experiences with the new doctor. When I was finished, she looked at me and said, "You are really f*****d up, we need to get you some help." I was told I needed to get some help through the Mental Health Department. She left the room, came back and literally grabbed my hand and walked me through the back hallways to another office. For lack of a better name, it was in the triage office of the Mental Health Department. This is where I had to prove what level of help, if any, I needed and deserved.

Again, I told this person everything! Now let me tell you, before this person began our little session, she stated that to get into the mental health counseling process is usually about a 6 to 8 month wait. After hearing all my issues, granted I was very personal and candid with her, she said, "Okay, you are really messed up. We need to get you some help." She looked in her calendar and asked, "How does this Thursday work?"

I really was in the right place at the right time. Timing is everything. "Cool, I'm in." And so it began.

At the appointed time, I walked into the Mental Health Department and went to the desk for my appointment. The person behind the desk gave me the famous huge stack of papers to fill out, that I have done a hundred times, I hated to do this again. I walked over to a chair, sat down, and began to fill out the mundane paperwork.

I was not done with the second page when a woman walked up to me and asked, "Are you Blair Hope?" I looked up, smiled, and said, "Yes, I am." She quickly replied, with her own smile, "Good, I will take that." I told her I wasn't finished filling it out. "No worries, I will take care of this," she said, still smiling. "You are in the wrong area. Let's take you upstairs to the PTSD orientation." Off we went.

She escorted me to a room with six other men in the room. I sat down and filled out another form and gave it back. Then walked in Miss Smith. Miss Smith was a Navy veteran herself and clearly knew her business in the PTSD Mental Health realm. Miss Smith began to welcome us and explain the three different levels of therapy. Basically, soft, medium, and hardcore 12-week therapy sessions. After a few identifying questions, it was obvious which course I would take. After the orientation was finished, I approached her and stated that the course I wanted was the hardcore 12- week session. She looked at me and agreed. I then asked her if she had availability to fit me in her schedule. She stated that her schedule was completely full and she would not be able to take me on as a client. After she asked me a few more personal probing questions, she again looked at her calendar, told me she wanted to take me on as a patient and fit me into her schedule the very next week. "How does next Thursday sound," she asked.

The following week we began our 12-week PTSD therapy sessions. Wow, talk about a journey into vulnerability!

The following Thursday, we embarked on the journey of what they call Prolonged Exposure Therapy for PTSD.

What is Post-Traumatic Stress Disorder (PTSD)?

PTSD is an anxiety that may develop after people experience or witness an event that involved actual or perceived threat to life or physical injury. The person's emotional reaction to such events is characterized by horror, terror, and helplessness. People experience PTSD through types of symptoms including:

- Re-experiencing the trauma.
- Avoiding trauma reminders.
- Emotional numbness.
- Hyperarousal

Hyperarousal occurs when a person's body suddenly kicks into high alert as a result of triggers of their trauma. Even though real danger may not be present, their body acts as if it is, causing lasting stress after a traumatic event.

Traumatic events commonly result in these kinds of difficulties immediately after experiencing them but do not necessarily mean that they have PTSD. For a majority of people, the frequency and intensity of these symptoms decrease over time as a part of a natural recovery. Some people, however, do not experience a decrease in these symptoms, resulting in chronic distress that can interfere with daily functioning.

What is Prolonged Exposure Therapy?

Prolonged Exposure Therapy is a systematic and direct way to help people who have experienced trauma to emotionally process their experiences and reduce the trauma-related problems. This therapy is based on decades of research in treating anxiety-related disorders and has established a high level of evidence about its effectiveness.

The main principle behind this therapy is the safe exposure to anxiety-producing situations in a way that allows people the time and the space to face these trauma memories and adapt to them. This is a powerful way for people to realize that situations or activities associated with trauma memories are not the same thing as trauma itself and allows people to safely remember trauma and experience trauma reminders. This is often associated with decreased anxiety and fear as well as an increased ability to tolerate anxiety.

Prolonged therapy includes several components:

- Education about common reactions to trauma.
- Breathing retraining.
- Repeated in vivo ("in real life") exposure to situations or activities that people are avoiding because they remind people of trauma experiences.
- Repeated, prolonged imaginary exposure to the trauma memories.

In vivo and imaginary exposures are the core of the treatment and have quite a bit of research supporting their use with PTSD as well as a variety of other anxiety disorders.

Emotional Processing Theory of PTSD

Prolonged Exposure Therapy is based on the Emotional Processing Theory of PTSD developed by Edna Foa and M.J. Kozak. This theory emphasizes that special processing of trauma must take place in order to reduce PTSD symptoms. It is based on the idea that fear is represented in your mind as a "program" for escaping danger. They named this program the "fear structure." The fear structure includes a variety of information and responses to possible threats and the relationship between threats and responses.

When fear in a given situation is realistic, we call it normal fear and the fear structure contains information about how we can best respond to the real threat. For example, if you see a mountain lion while hiking, acting to escape may be an appropriate response and can be seen as a normal and helpful fear reaction. But if you have the same reaction when seeing a mountain lion in a zoo, this is not an adaptive reaction. For those with PTSD, the fear structure is activated too frequently and too intensely in situations that are relatively safe.

The fear structure becomes a problem when:

- The information in the structure does not accurately represent the world.

- Physical and escape/avoidance responses are triggered by harmless stimuli.

- The fear responses interfere with daily functioning.

- Harmless stimuli and responses are viewed as being dangerous.

The goal of interventions to address problems with the fear structure involve helping people adjust their fear structure so it is more adaptive in more situations. This is done by "activating" this programming in safe situations. Once activated, realistic information needs to replace the original, unrealistic information in the fear structure (for example: I will fall apart if I allow myself to talk or think about the trauma). Think of this as editing a document in a computer. You cannot make changes unless you open the document file first.

Emotional Processing Theory describes chronic PTSD as the failure to process trauma memory fully. So the goal of therapy is to promote and encourage this. Safe exposure to feared stimuli results in activation (bringing to mind) of the relevant fear structure and at the same time provides realistic information about the likelihood and cost of the consequences of this fear. In addition to the fear of external threat (for example, being attacked again), the person may have unhelpful or inaccurate beliefs about the anxiety itself that are disconfirmed during exposure. Such as the belief that the anxiety will never end until the situation is escaped or that the anxiety will cause the person to "lose control" or "go crazy." This new information is learned during the exposure session, which changes the fear structure and causes the person to be less afraid the next time he or she faces that situation, and thereby results in a reduction of PTSD symptoms.

Prolonged Exposure Therapy for the treatment of PTSD works by bringing to mind the fear structure, deliberately confronting trauma-related thoughts and images, imaginal and in vivo exposure, and learning what people are afraid of is very unlikely to happen.

By confronting trauma memories and reminders, people learn that they can tolerate these situations and that nothing bad happens to them. They also learn that their anxiety will decrease even while they are confronting what they fear. People learn that they do not go crazy or lose control. Imaginal and in vivo exposure exercises help people tell the difference between the traumatic event and other similar but non-dangerous events. This allows people to see the trauma as a specific event occurring in the space and time, which helps them get over the feelings and thoughts that the world is entirely dangerous and that they are completely incompetent to deal with it.

People with PTSD often report that thinking about the traumatic event makes it feel as if it is happening all over again. Repeated imaginal exposure to the trauma memory tells people the difference between people of the past and present. It helps them realize that although remembering the trauma can be emotionally upsetting, the trauma is not happening again and therefore thinking about the event is not dangerous. Repeating imaginal exposure also helps people think differently about what happened to them.

The structure of the Prolonged Exposure Therapy was absolutely imperative in my healing, learning to process, acknowledge, accept, and file my memories. My therapy lasted twelve sessions. During my sessions, we covered proper breathing and meditation techniques. We covered the common problems after trauma. Such as: fear and anxiety, increased arousal, avoidance, anger and irritability, feelings of guilt and shame, grief and depression, self-image and views of the world, sexual relationships, alcohol and other substance use.

We also discussed Subjective Units of Discomfort (SUDS). Each session included weekly homework assignments, consisting of those units of discomfort, listening to the recorded trauma incidents, being in crowds of people, right in the middle of them, not sitting on the side wall with my back to the room, observing everything, being in a constant Yellow Condition awareness setting. Watching movies with helicopter sounds and crashes. Viewing pictures of caskets draped with the flag of the United States in a hangar bay.

This in vivo exposure to two of the main trauma incidents I encountered was absolutely amazing. The emotions, vulnerability, and pain I had to re-live was difficult, but absolutely imperative to the healing process.

The next exercise or object lesson my therapist took me through was priceless. Miss Smith put it like this: "Blair, here is your problem. You have all these memories of your traumatic events in your head that you have compartmentalized. But the problem is, you don't know how to, or refuse to, acknowledge, and accept them, by storing them away properly."

She told me that she was a very organized person and therapist, and others were very messy and not so organized. If you sat in her office, you would know exactly what she was talking about. Everything was in order, and everything had its place. You see Blair, I am very organized. She pulls out her file cabinet drawer, every file folder labeled, neat and orderly.

"You see Blair, I can take this folder right here, your folder, full of all your traumatic events, the blood, the bodies, the helicopter crash. I can view them, look at them, remember them. Knowing they are right there. They are not going to go away, you cannot forget them, the memories, the emotions, or the pain. But I can see them all organized, acknowledge them, and accept them. And then, I can close that folder with all of those memories, and I can place that folder back in that organized file cabinet drawer, then close that drawer, knowing that all those memories are still there, they are not going to go away, and I can revisit them anytime I want. That is what you need to do Blair," she explained.

For some reason, that object lesson made me so angry, I even called her a flavorful name, which I later apologized for, and she understood.

That was my problem. I was afraid to acknowledge, accept, and file those memories. I had been taught to compartmentalize so well, even from a small child. My walls were so thick. They became so thick and weak at the same time, they imploded, they crumbled around me and inside me. The way to repair them was to acknowledge what they were, the damage they had done, and the pain they had caused. Taking those remains and forming more building blocks, organizing, and storing them away properly. Wow, what a novel idea. I am now able to share that story with others, without going through pain and suffering. That is not something I could do before my therapy.

Again, I tell you, that I am nobody special. But if someone can learn from my experiences to help themselves, then we both win.

I must give a huge shout out to my therapist, Annika Smith, VA Salt Lake City, Utah. I could not have done this without her. Her persistence and patience in dealing with me for 12 weeks was so valuable. After successfully completing the Prolonged Exposure Therapy sessions, Miss Smith awarded me with a challenge coin made for those veterans who completed the course. "Wow," I said, "you must have given quite a few of these out."

"No," she said, "you are the first. It may only be a challenge coin to you, but it was a reward for a completion of a milestone that was long overdue."

As mentioned in Chapter 4 concerning the helicopter crash and the loss of eight great men, do you have what it takes to move on? Yes, you do! You must move on for them, but more than that, you need to move on for you and your posterity.

I just want to hear the words "I am proud of you." Well, I am proud of you! By reading this book, I know you are taking your first step in the right direction to believe in yourself and know that others believe in you as well.

There is "HOPE."
God does give "HOPE."

CHAPTER 8

Find People Who Genuinely Care

"The world belongs to those that show up."
—Blair D. Hope

I have always been told you must have an education to get a good job or career. I believed this wholeheartedly. But you see, I had this problem. A problem with illiteracy. And to make things worse, I could not comprehend what I read. I was in resource class until the 9th grade (a remedial class). As God would have it, I graduated from resource in the 9th grade.

You see, God does give "HOPE" in many sizes and shapes, and personages.

Every kid needs to learn from adult leaders who are willing to be mentors, or willing to rap a kid upside their head when needed. I have had some great men in my life teach me the rights and wrongs, guide me in the right direction, and pull me back from the wrong direction. These would include Rulon Fellows, my Scout Master when I was 11 years old. Rulon was kindhearted, taught us the basics of life survival, and wasn't afraid to rap you upside the head if you were not listening.

Dave Isom was a second dad to me. Very much a father figure in my youth. A wonderful man, stubborn and willing to go out of his way to look after me. Dave was the Scoutmaster who showed up at my house to take me to Scout camp and would not take no for an answer. He showed me what it meant to care for some kid that was not yours. He took me under his wing, and showed me a love, and a love for the Boy Scout program. He introduced me to the Order of the Arrow program, the National Honor Society of Scouting. He treated me as his own Son by proving to me that God has sent great men to look after those who need saving. Dave also introduced me to the Mountain Man Rendezvous culture, which is still a big part of my family's activities today.

Rudy Devries was one of the most caring, loving, forgiving men I have ever known. Rudy believed in me and inspired me to be all that I wanted to be. He helped me learn that the world was not out to get me, I was out to get the world. Rudy was my bishop right before I joined the Navy.

Tom Jackson was my best friend's dad. Tom was a man's man. He was a former Marine drill instructor and told you the way it was. But he also has a heart of gold. He made me feel like his own Son, and still does to this day.

This includes Mrs. Simmons, the resource teacher in junior high. I feel she was sent by God to save and improve my life. When I got into Mrs. Simmons' class, she asked me what I wanted to accomplish. I told her I wanted to read fast and normally like the rest of the kids. She said, "Okay, this is what we need to do." She not only told me what I needed to do, she read with me, timed me, tested me, over and over. For three years while in junior high, we worked hard. Then one day while in the 9th grade, she told me my test scores were high enough that I no longer needed to be in resource classes. I still struggle with English, grammar, and rhetoric, which has played out for the rest of my life. It gets better every day. Especially being married to a grammar Nazi. I love me wife dearly. She gets me through every day.

Mrs. Simmons' effect on my life did not stop there in the 9th grade. When I started high school, all I wanted to do, was to be a better person, scholastically as well as staying out of trouble. When you get in trouble in high school, you get called down to the office. When you really got in trouble you were sent to the counseling office. Well, one day in my sophomore year, I was called down to the office. As I entered the office to announce myself, they told me to report to the counseling office. As I entered the counseling office, I was told somebody was there to see me. WHAT!?! Who in the world wanted to see me?

I walked into the next room and there sat Mrs. Simmons. She was there to say hi and check on me and my progress. Who does that? She didn't have to do that, that wasn't her job. Wow! That is what true "HOPE" looks like. Caring enough for somebody else, sacrificing your personal time to check on one of your past students.

From then on, I was really trying to do well in school. My grades continued to get better and better. Graduating with a 3.5 grade point average.

Mrs. Simmons checked on me during my sophomore, junior, and senior years at Taylorsville High School. Her gift of "HOPE" kept giving.

Her actions were truly the foundation of how I have lived the rest of my life and the various activities and community programs I was involved in. I have always strived to look after people to help build them up. Mrs. Simmons was the epitome of servanthood leadership.

Education is the process of facilitating learning for the acquisition of knowledge, skills, values, morals, beliefs, and habits. Educational methods include teaching, training, storytelling, discussion and directed research. Education frequently takes place under the guidance of educators. However, learners can also educate themselves. Education can take place in a formal and informal setting and any experience that has a formative effect on the way one thinks, feels, and acts may be considered educational.

Having a degree, knowledge, and subject matter is not enough to get you a good job or career. It is how you apply yourself with that knowledge and education. It is how you present yourself to others. It is how you close the deal. It is how you ask for that job or career. This later would lead to one of my favorite sayings and methods of execution, "marketing and exposure."

I lacked money, somebody of influence, or a scholarship, so I quickly came to believe that a higher education was not in the cards for me.

During the last half of my senior year, I applied for several scholarships and did not hear anything back from those colleges during the same time frame my friends were receiving their scholarships. I was living with my grandfather at the time, and I knew I couldn't stay with him forever. I didn't know what to do.

My best friend, Andy Jackson, joined the Navy Reserves. He went to boot camp during the summer of his junior year in high school. I thought it was cool. I knew I could not join the Navy Reserves, because what was I going to do, go to boot camp and come back and live with my grandfather again, NO! I decided to join the Navy full time. I was still in high school and I was only 17 years old. My mom had to sign papers allowing me to enlist in the Navy because I was not 18. I couldn't attend boot camp until the summer after graduation, so I had to enlist into the (DEP) Delayed Entry Program for six months. I was so excited to see the world.

Well, things got a little interesting from there. I received three scholarships, well two partial scholarships and one full scholarship without housing. Man, I really wanted to go to college, and I also wanted to serve a mission for my church. I went to the Navy Recruiter, a Chief Petty Officer, and told him I wanted to get out of the DEP program, go to college, and serve a mission for my church. He said sure, we can let you out with a dishonorable discharge. No thank you! Not for me. I didn't want a blemish like that on my record forever. Especially since my father was given a BCD (Big Chicken Dinner or Bad Conduct Discharge).

I later found out that the Chief Petty Officer had lied to me. I could have gotten out of the DEP program. He told me that since I had already been sworn in and had taken the Oath, I could not get out of the DEP program. Truth be known, you don't officially swear in and take the Oath until you are processed through the MEPS (Military Entrance Processing Station) before you are shipped off to Boot Camp. I found this to be true when I had the opportunity to serve my community with the HARP (Home Area Recruiting Program).

It's always good to receive letters of appreciation. Below is a letter Aaron Hooley and I received from our high school teacher while serving on HARP duty.

June 6, 1990

To Whom it May Concern:

*AN Blair D. Hope and HN Aaron Hooley, former
students of mine returned to Taylorsville High School in
their uniforms and spoke to my students. They informed
the students of the excellent career benefits, educational
opportunities, and technical skills that the navy
furnishes its people. Also, pay, naval programs, and how
the reserves would benefit a young man were discussed.*

*It is obvious that Blair and Aaron are a credit to the
Navy. My students were impressed by what they said and
how they looked in their uniforms. It was obvious by
what was discussed that the Armed Forces have become
highly technical and professional.*

Sincerely,

Richard W. Haight
Teacher, Taylorsville H.S.

It all worked out for the best. I joined the Navy, and it was the best
thing I ever did. It changed my life. It gave me the confidence, disciplines,
attitudes, strategic planning, situational awareness are all immeasurable
attributes that have made me the man I am today.

I will never forget the day I heard the song "I Still Believe," sung
by Tim Capello in the movie Lost Boys. Awesome song! The movie had
a good plot as well. How bad somebody wants to fit in, but realizes he
had to fight to get out and do what was right. How many of us can relate
to that? Knowing that our own decisions have placed us in our current
situations. Realizing what we must do to correct and/or get out of those
situations. Do you still believe? Do you believe in yourself?

"God does give HOPE."

Another testament of that is a man called Steve "Spice" Spicer. One
of the best men and brothers I would ever have. Spice is the epitome of

what a mentor, leader, manager, friend, and brother should be. Spice took a chance on me and enabled my career with Procter & Gamble (P&G). He hired me with no college degree, even though Procter & Gamble pretty much insisted on a master's degree. Because I had a proven track record during a beta test adventure P&G was trying with a part time merchandising company.

Spice mentored me, trained me, and introduced me to the book "Managing Your Mouth." I learned what it meant to have a clearing, through the ministry "Marked Men for Christ" (MMFC). Spice was a man of tough love. He was extremely competitive by nature but managed it with finesse. So when talking about a man sacrificing his time and efforts to improve another man, God does give "HOPE," and he sent an archangel, one called Steve "Spice" Spicer.

I attended my first college course while I was on my first deployment in the Navy. They flew out an instructor from the University of Phoenix to teach us an English/public speaking class. When I returned stateside, I continued my college education at Chapman College via telecourses. Talk about having to be disciplined. All the classes were recorded on VHS tapes. I was stuck in a room by myself watching the college course tapes, I would do the essays and homework, send it to the instructor on campus in Orange, CA and await his reply. When I got out of the Navy, I continued my college courses and degree at the Salt Lake Community College and Utah State University. It took me ten years to get my associates degree in business.

The key here is that I didn't give up. It was a long, challenging 10 years of hard work and study. I had a goal, and nothing was going to stop me. I did it!

I would never tell anyone that going to college is not important. However, do not let the lack of a degree stop you. You do not need a formal education to be successful and have a career. You do need to have an education. How you receive that education is up to you. Find a way to educate yourself, but more importantly, find a way to apply what you learn.

Make yourself valuable and promotion worthy. Enable and empower yourself to be set up for success. Learn to market yourself, and your added value, to the world.

There is "HOPE."
God does give "HOPE."

CHAPTER 9

Enabling and Empowering Others' Passions and Talents

"The person who knows how will always have a job, but the person who knows why will always be the boss."
—Blair D. Hope

Passions and talents. Two of my favorite words. But more importantly, my favorite way to observe and manage people.

When managing people, we are often told to use this person for that position, or you can't use that person for that position. In my experience, when utilizing my passions and talents theory, I choose to observe differently. I believe people show up for a reason, and it is usually some sort of passion or talent. I believe that when assigning jobs or tasks to people, you should look for those that have a passion or talent for the task. I believe that when a person is tasked with a job they have a passion for, you will gain 30 percent more productivity from them simply because they want to do the job, and they enjoy doing it.

Learn the passions and talents of others. People show up for a reason. It is your job to find out their passions and talents and put them to work where they can put those passions and talents to use.

People can be very annoying, overconfident, arrogant, introverted, extroverted, or different in many other ways. Those same people can be very valuable and offer many talents to your group - through their passions. Are you able to accept those passions and talents and excuse the rest?

I work with many people across the board that just drive me crazy. But I can accept their help, enable, and empower them in the right direction to have a win-win situation in the groups I work with.

I learned a very valuable lesson from the Executive Officer (XO) of the USS Okinawa LPH-3. I was notified that I was to receive a Commendation Medal from a Personnel Petty Officer 1st Class. I told him that was great and to please just file it into my personnel record. The next thing I knew, I got a message to report to the XO's stateroom. When I arrived, he welcomed me in saying: "Petty Officer Hope, I understand we have a problem?" He then explained: "I understand that you do not want to be publicly recognized and receive your Commendation Medal?"

I told him that he was correct. I said: "I feel I did my job. I appreciate the recognition and placing it into my personnel record is adequate."

"I understand and respect you for what you are saying", he said, "but you need to understand that it is not just about you. It is just as important, if not more important, that your command and subordinates see you receive this commendation medal. They need to see that you can be recognized for going above and beyond the call of duty."

I told him that I now understood. I was later awarded that commendation medal, in front of the entire command. I must admit, it did feel good to be publicly recognized.

Something else I learned, was to never be afraid to make connections, regardless of the outcome. During an operation in Saudi Arabia, I connected with a Saudi Arabian Officer, while I was a non-commissioned officer in the Navy. We happened to get on the topic of his religion and mine, and I learned that he was Muslim. He later contacted me, by visiting me on the USS Okinawa. He was waiting on the quarterdeck of the ship while I was notified of his arrival. We visited briefly and he gave me a paper bag with gifts inside. He gifted me a Quran, the text of his religion, and other printed material about the Muslim religion. Now that drew some attention. Not only did a Saudi Arabian Officer come to visit a U.S. Naval ship, he came to visit a non-commissioned officer, and gave him a gift in a paper brown bag.

I was questioned by my Division Chief Petty Officer, the Department Air Commander, and the Command Executive Officer. They asked, why did he come to visit you? What is your relationship? What did he give you? Why would an officer come to visit an enlisted man? It was all very amusing to me. Why should it matter? Well, this sort of thing was unusual, and they had security concerns. I learned early on to make connections everywhere. The network and relations you build with people throughout your life will be the most priceless tool and resource you will ever have.

Years ago, I adopted a slogan that I have applied to my professional and volunteer career. "It is my job to make you look good, and by default, I look good." How true this is in everything we do. In the professional world, this can be used both with your upper management teams and with those that you manage. In the volunteer world, it is very valuable as you manage different teams with a holistic goal.

When you enable and empower people to be successful in your group, they not only receive the blessings and benefits of that success, but you also look good as their leader or manager. It behooves you to do all you can to make them look good. Sometimes that may require helping them to do their work, maybe even completing some of it for them. They will see your genuine support and strive to look good themselves.

This leads to charisma. I like this definition:

"How can you have charisma? Be more concerned about making others feel good about themselves than you are making them feel good about you."—Dan Reiland

Most people think of charisma as being something mystical, almost undefinable. They think it is a quality that comes at birth, or not at all. I don't believe that is true. Charisma, plainly stated, is the ability to draw people to you. Like other character traits, it can be developed.

To make yourself the kind of person who attracts others, to become attractive and contagious, you need to consider a few things.

You must love life. People enjoy the company of leaders who enjoy life. Think of people you want to spend time with. How would you describe them? Ornery? Sour? Depressed? Of course not. They're celebrators, not complainers. They're passionate about life. If you want to attract people, you need to be like the people you enjoy being with.

Everyone starts with an "A," as in the movie, "Dangerous Minds." An ex-Marine turned teacher (Michelle Pfeiffer) struggled to connect with her students in an inner- city school until she adopted the philosophy that "everyone starts with an 'A.' It's their job to keep it."

Another way to look at it is to put an "A" on every person's head. One of the best things you can do for people, which attracts them to you, is to think the best of them and from them. It helps others to think more highly of themselves, and at the same time, it also helps you.

Give people "Hope." Napoleon Bonaparte characterized leaders as "dealers of hope." Like all great leaders, he knew that hope is the greatest of all possessions. If you can be a person that bestows that gift onto others, they will be attracted to you, and they will be forever grateful.

Share yourself. People love leaders who share themselves and their life's journey. As you lead people, give of yourself. Share wisdom, resources, and even special occasions. That's one of my favorite things to do. I love to share stories of my children, my travels, and experiences.

When it comes to charisma, the bottom line is othermindedness. Leaders who think about others and their concerns before thinking of themselves exhibit charisma. "It is my job to make you look good, by default, I look good."

Even if you don't have your sights on leading the country, as Ronald Reagan did, you still need to possess the ability to communicate. The success of your marriage, job, and personal relationships depends greatly on it. People will not follow you if they don't know what you want, or where you are going. I have learned the value of competence, which is the ability to do something successfully or efficiently.

Competence is more than words. If you want to display high competence, here is what you need to do.

Show up every day. There's a saying, "All things come to those who wait." Unfortunately, sometimes all that comes to them are leftovers from the people who got there first. Responsible people show up when they're expected. But highly competent people take it a step farther. They don't show up in body only. They come ready to play the game every day, no matter how they feel, what kind of circumstances they face, or how difficult they expect the game to be. Show up!

Keep Improving. All highly competent people continually search for ways to keep learning, growing, and improving. They do that by asking: "Why?" I used to drive people crazy by always asking why. After all, the person who knows how will always have a job, but the person who knows why will always be the boss.

Follow through and execute with excellence. This was a tough lesson for me to learn. I have never met a person I considered competent who didn't follow through. I bet it's the same for you.

"Quality is never an accident. It is always the result of high intention, sincere effort, intelligent direction and skillful execution. It represents the wise choice of many alternatives," said Willa A. Foster.

Performing at a high level of excellence is always a choice, an act of will. As leaders, we expect our people to follow through when we hand them the ball. They expect that, and a whole lot more from us as leaders.

Accomplish more than expected. My old manager, Dave Sick, always had a saying, "plus 2." Always plan to hit your goal, plus 2 more. I would submit to you, that if you focus on the "plus 2," hitting your goal becomes a little easier. Thanks Dave Sick.

Highly competent people always go the extra mile. For them, good enough is never good enough. In "Men in Mid-Life Crisis," Jim Conway writes that some people feel "a weakening of the need to be a great man and an increasing feeling of let's just get through this the best we can." Many have the attitude: "Never mind hitting home runs. Let's just get through the ball game without getting beaned." Leaders cannot afford to have that kind of attitude. They need to do the job, and then do even more and make it a "plus 2."

Inspire others. Highly competent leaders do more than perform at a high level. They inspire and motivate their people to do the same. While some people rely on relational skills alone to survive, effective leaders combine these skills with high competence to take their organizations to new levels of excellence and influence. When it comes to having more insight on influencing people, I highly recommend reading "How to Win Friends and Influence People" by Dale Carnegie.

Generosity. Nothing speaks more loudly than the generosity of a leader. True generosity isn't an occasional event. It comes from the heart and permeates every aspect of a leader's life, touching his time, money, talents, and possessions. Effective leaders, the kind that people want to follow, don't gather things just for themselves, they do it to give to others.

Cultivate the quality of generosity in your life. How?

Be grateful for what you have. It's hard for people to be generous when they are not satisfied with what they have. Generosity arises out of gratitude, and that doesn't come with acquiring more. It comes from genuinely being happy and grateful for what you have.

Be grateful for the people you serve. Put people first. The measure of a leader is not the number who serve them, but the number of people they serve. Generosity requires putting others first. If you can do that, giving becomes much easier.

I will always be forever grateful to my grandfather, Parley A. Sargent. He is my hero. He taught me many lessons in life and how to survive. One of the profound lessons I learned was about true success. One day he asked me if I knew the true definition of "Success." Oh man, I had this one. You see, my grandfather, in my mind, was a very successful man. He was a great man who worked hard to provide for his family, retired from the sheet metal union, had money sufficient for his needs and a comfortable lifestyle, and he outlived two beautiful wives. Any man would be happy with his worldly possessions.

I knew the answer. I told him the definition of success was his lifestyle, the big house, truck and trailer, money in the bank, enough to travel where he wanted. All material things. He listened to me until I was finished, paused for a moment, then very prophetically told me I was WRONG. Wow, what? I was wrong? He told me that the true definition of success had nothing to do with all the material things. The true definition of success was the amount of people surrounding you while on your death bed. Now reflect on that.

Don't allow the desire for possessions to control you. According to Earle Wilson, people can be divided into three groups: "Haves, have-nots, and have not paid for what they have." More and more people are becoming enslaved to the desire to acquire. Author Richard Foster writes. "Owning things is an obsession in our culture. If we own it, we feel we can control it. And if we can control it, we feel it will give us more pleasure. The idea is an illusion."

"If you want to be in charge of your heart, don't allow possessions to take charge of you." —Blair D. Hope

Develop a habit of giving. Andrew Carnegie wrote an essay called "Gospel of Wealth." In it he said that the life of a wealthy person should have two periods. A time of acquiring wealth and one of redistributing it. The only way to maintain an attitude of generosity is to make it your habit to give – your time, attention, money, and resources. Obviously, we all don't have the wealth of Andrew Carnegie, but we do have the same precious resource, time. To be generous, you can give freely of your time. If you are enslaved by greed, you cannot lead.

We always have the choice to give of our time. Another phrase that I like to use, "You always have time for what you want to do." I like to refer to this as servanthood.

Servanthood is not about position or skill, it's about attitude. What does it mean to embody the quality of servanthood?

Put others ahead of your own agenda. The first sign of servanthood is the ability to put others ahead of yourself and your personal desires. It is more than being willing to put your agenda on hold for a minute. It means intentionally being aware of your people's needs, be available to help them, and be able to accept their desires and needs as important.

Possess the confidence to serve. The real heart of servanthood is confidence. Show me someone who is too important to serve others, and

I'll show you someone who lacks confidence. How we treat others really reflects how we think about ourselves.

"The Law of Empowerment says that only secure leaders give power to others. It's also true that only secure leaders exhibit servanthood." —John C. Maxwell

Initiate service to others. Just about anyone will serve if compelled to do so. Some will serve in a crisis. You can really see the heart of someone who initiates service to others. Great leaders see the need, seize the opportunity, and serve without expecting anything in return.

Don't be position conscious. Servant leaders don't focus on rank or position. When Colonel Norman Schwarzkopf stepped into the minefield, rank was the last thing on his mind. He was one person trying to help another. If anything, being the leader gave him a greater sense of obligation to serve.

Serve out of love. Servanthood is not motivated by manipulation or self-promotion. It is fueled by love. In the end, the extent of your influence depends on the depth of your concern for others. That's why it is so important for leaders to be willing to serve. Are you a servant leader?

Have you ever had somebody believe in you more than you believed in yourself? I told you about Mrs. Simmons, my resource teacher in junior high school. There was Mr. Haight, my psychology teacher. He believed in me so much. He knew I could go on to do something great in my life.

When I went home as a Home Area Recruiter, part of the HARP (Home Area Recruiting Program), I was able to speak to his psychology class at Taylorsville High School about being in the Navy and what benefits it offered. Mr. Haight would later write a letter of appreciation and recommendation on my behalf to the United States Navy.

How I wish I could find Mrs. Simmons and Mr. Height today and share my gratitude with them and show how thankful I am for their time and sacrifices they offered me.

It's not only teachers or adults that can enable others and give confidence. I will always be forever grateful for Becky Tanner. One of those girls who was out of my league. Becky believed in me. She knew my history and challenges to overcome my inability to read. She loved reading books. I loved to hear her stories from the books she had read.

She knew how to relate those stories while delivering very moving church talks in Sacrament meetings (Sunday meetings of The Church of Jesus Christ of Latter-day Saints).

When I left for the Navy, she gave me a stack of books. I read them all, and that led to my love for reading books. I was once told that you can travel the world by reading books, and you really can.

I loved reading about history. I fell in love with the Louis L'Amour books. I have read almost all of his 250 books. I remember going on many scavenger hunts, trading with U.S. Marines in our command, and other Navy sailors to obtain as many Louis L'Amour books I could get my hands on.

I believe the reason I was so fascinated with his books, was that they were so detailed with the surroundings of where the stories of the books were taking place. Louis L'Amour's books were fictional, but the places he wrote about were real. He wrote about the places he visited, worked, or had experience with. I loved his book "Education of Wandering Man." He was a traveling hobo, not a bum. A man who worked as he traveled.

In some sort of weird way, I found myself relating with Louis L'Amour. I could relate to many of the places that were in his books. He often wrote about places in my home state of Utah, or the west.

By reading many books, I enabled myself to read faster, articulate their stories, build confidence, and comprehend many topics of interest.

Your youth or your past does not have to define you, it describes what you have gone through. You define your future by your attitude, actions, and your goals. Act now!

Teamwork

There is no I in TEAM. But is that really true? You are the "I." You are in TEAM, or you should want to be. The question is, how do you prepare and transform yourself to be part of the TEAM?

When we were born, God gave us small feet, which left a very small footprint, enough for somebody else to identify with.

As we grew older, our feet grew as well. Enough that we could be identified by the imprint of our feet.

But as we grow old, our footprint is only the size of our feet, which stopped growing.

God has given us the ability to enable and empower others. The more love and encouragement we share, the larger the footprint gets. Our footprint can have a large impact far bigger than just the size of our physical feet.

Don't settle for the size of your feet, make a bigger footprint by the way you serve others. Imagine the size it could be.

What is your legacy going to look like?

There is "HOPE."
God does give "HOPE."

CHAPTER 10

Are You Good Enough?

*"What man is there that does not want
to make the world better?"*
—Blair D. Hope

I did not feel I was ever good enough at anything when I was young. Even though I knew, deep down inside, I was just as good as others.

Be Competitive

I always told my kids that they had to do something competitive. I wanted them to have a sense of the reality in the world, because the world is very competitive. "You can do anything you want if you put your mind to it. Just be your best," I told them.

I love the story of my sons, Dalton and Bridger. My boys are studs. Both were good baseball players. When Dalton was in high school, he was a great baseball player and could have gone far in the sport. He also played the trumpet in the school marching band and was on the ballroom dance team. One day he came to me and asked, "Dad, do you care if I stop playing baseball? I want to focus on my trumpet playing and ballroom dancing."

"What have I always told you," I asked.

He stated how I always said he had to do something competitive. I asked if playing in the Marching Band was competitive, and he said, "I think so."

Are you kidding me? There's no question. The year before, the marching band at Tooele High School, was the only team in the school to bring home a state trophy. The marching band has two practices a day. Early morning before school, and then after school practices. They are a team, a team that works hard and competes together, improving throughout the year. I told Dalton, focusing on playing the trumpet in the marching band was indeed competitive. Dalton and Bridger were both state and nationally ranked in band and ballroom dancers. I am very proud of them both. I am proud of all my children.

I never thought I was good enough as a kid, even though I excelled above others. I quit everything as a kid because I never felt good enough or supported. I quit baseball, the game I loved so much, because I felt I didn't fit in. I was good at baseball, and I quit. I quit wrestling because I didn't feel I was good enough. How I longed for a big brother, or more, a father.

I remember when I was in the fifth grade, we were out playing kickball on the playground. I had a couple of awesome kicks which scored several runs. We were in the field. There was huge applause for a popular kid, because he had a great kick to the outfield. When I had an awesome throw to second base to get that guy out, not a word was said - deafening. Suddenly Mr. Woods, our fifth-grade teacher, was yelling. He asked why everybody cheered for the popular kid when he had a great kick, but no one said anything to the kid who got the popular kid out with a great throw. He gave a speech on inclusiveness. That really felt good, I wish I could have hung on to that feeling forever.

The absolute best thing God did for me, was to enable my path to the United States Navy. There I learned and embraced confidence. I learned that what others thought and felt about me did not matter when it came to my personal development and progress. Yes, I continued to have, and still have, issues with self-worth, but I have learned to channel them.

If you have not read the book, "The Traveler's Gift," by Andy Andrews, I highly recommend that you place it on your must-read list. I don't believe you will find a better self-help book. It will help you find yourself coming out on top and having a better positive attitude as you approach the reality of life. Realizing you can make a difference in your life as well as others. You do make a difference!

Yes, you are good enough!

Who are you? What are you made of? Do you have character?

Character is more than talk. Talk is cheap. Anyone can say that they have integrity, but actions are the real indicator of character. Actions speak louder than words. Your character determines who you are. Who you are determines what you see. What you see determines what you do. That's why you can never separate a leader's character from their actions. If a leader's actions and intentions are continually working against each other, then look to their character and find out why.

Talent is a gift, but character is a choice. We have no control over a lot of things in life. We don't get to choose our parents. We don't get to select the location or circumstances of our birthplace and upbringing. We don't get to pick our talents or IQ. But we do choose our character. We create it every time we make choices. To give up or to dig down deep to come out of a hard situation. To bend the truth or own the weight of it. To take the easy road or the road less traveled. As you live your life, making choices every day, you will continue to create your own character.

These stories I share in this book are not meant to be "pity poor me" stories, they are to show you that we can overcome anything we want, as long as we want. Yes, we may have some long-term issues and effects, but we can still choose how to respond to them and how they affect us.

Once You Know You are Good Enough...

I was once called a Change Agent. I had progressed from being uncertain that I was good enough to someone who could bring about change.

Change agents inspire and lead change processes at their jobs and in their industries. Through formal and informal leadership, they may seek to increase employee satisfaction, optimize organizational efficiency and increase an organization's abilities to meet its goals. Understanding what they do and why they're valuable to companies can help you decide if you want to be a change agent in your field or at your company.

What is a change agent?

A change agent is an action-oriented leader who seeks to improve the logistical, technical and interpersonal functions of an organization by changing policies, systems, processes or operational norms. They communicate why something is a problem, generate specific ideas for change and identify individuals to implement changes with them.

By taking initiative and showing leadership, Change Agents may give colleagues the confidence to also initiate change. For example, colleagues may decide to join a current project or develop their own changes to improve the organization.

Change Agents have specific ideas for change.

Change agents typically have a plan for specific changes they want to implement in an organization, including big and small details for a final product and a change process. They have specific ideas to build an action plan, stay organized, and lead others. They can describe their ideas to colleagues to help them build support for the desired change.

Change Agents have strong interpersonal skills.

Change Agents have strong people skills, including the ability to build and maintain relationships, communicate effectively, demonstrate empathy and provide constructive criticism. These skills can enable them to understand the impact of an organization's systems and processes on its employees, which can result in more informed decision-making and stronger leadership. They can use their interpersonal skills to explain the importance of changes to their colleagues and build peer support for a proposed change.

Change agents are willing to challenge ideas.

Being a Change Agent may involve taking some risks, such as challenging ideas or making suggestions that may not be popular with peers or supervisors. Change agents can consider the potential benefit to the organization and its employees when determining when and how to take risks. They can also prepare for challenging situations by creating backup plans. Being willing to take risks for the benefit of the organization may help build respect from colleagues and help advance needed change.

Change Agents must have flexibility with processes.

Changing processes can often be complex, so having flexibility is important for Change Agents. When confronted with obstacles, they may adjust their strategies or find alternative solutions. For example, if they encounter challenges when trying to change the educational requirements for prospective new employees, they may work with the human resources department to identify alternative solutions. Together, they might make changes such as adjusting other required qualifications or adjusting company recruitment strategies to attract candidates with diverse professional backgrounds and skill sets.

Change Agents need industry expertise.

Regardless of what professional industry they work in, Change Agents need to understand how their industry works and how to organize and implement systems, policies and structures. This includes knowledge of employee-facing systems like hiring, termination, performance reviews and benefits. It also includes knowledge of operations such as budgeting, teaming structure, contracting and procurement. With this knowledge, they can make informed recommendations that may help improve the organization while adhering to industry regulations.

Develop your skills as a Change Agent.

There are specific skills that can help you to be successful as a Change Agent, such as passion, initiative, analysis, critical thinking, problem-solving, planning and communication. There are a number of ways to develop these skills.

Observe your environment.

Start your development process by observing your current work environment and noting areas you want to change. This can help you develop skills in data collection, analysis, and critical thinking. Keeping formal records, informal notes or tracking pieces of information about a certain challenge may help ensure you're prepared when it's time to implement change. Observing the change and decision-making culture of your work environment, including which change strategies are effective, can also prepare you to initiate change.

Learn from your peers.

Whether in a personal or professional environment, learning from other Change Agents can help you develop your own skills. Examine how other Change Agents create or change policies in organizations, noting how they suggest new methods of doing things. Observing their approaches, successes, failures and techniques can help you build similar skills.

Practice on a small scale.

Making changes on a small scale can allow you to develop strategies and analyze results before making larger changes. This can also give you the opportunity to learn from potential mistakes. You can begin by testing changes within your own team and then deciding if you want to implement these changes at the organizational level. For example, if you want to change the form of communication the company uses, you might test out new communication strategies with smaller groups before implementing change within the entire company.

Seek feedback from others.

Seeking and incorporating feedback from trusted peers, mentors or supervisors who understand the change management process is a great way to develop your skills. Asking for specific feedback can help them provide you with helpful, actionable advice. For example, rather than asking general questions about your overall performance, you might ask for feedback specifically about the effectiveness of your communication in reaching diverse audiences. A Change Agent is the summary product of:

- Attitude, Dreams and Goals
- Assess-Adapt-Overcome
- Staying the Course
- Marketing and Exposure
- Persistency and Consistency
- Do you have what it takes?
- School of Hard Knocks
- Enabling and Empowering
- Are you good enough?

Reflect and ask yourself, are you the person that is ready to be your own Change Agent? Do you have a specific idea you want to implement at work or in a group you belong too? Are you willing to challenge ideas and be flexible with the process? Are you willing to set back, listen, and observe the environment? Learn from your peers and seek their feedback? If you are, put it into action, right now! In my particular situation, I was able to observe an organization for quite some time, stepping back with patience (which was very hard), noting my concerns, challenge traditions, seek feedback from others, compile data, design a plan, and present that plan to the key decision maker of the program, who was able to validate my data and concerns, and then made a decision for the future benefit of the program. I was able to be the advisor for that program for three years, weathering it through some very tragic times, that threatened the integrity, quality, and future of the program. We were able to maintain just over par level membership levels during three years in the face of decisions and actions I did not control. All because I wanted to see some positive change and was willing to challenge current ideas for the betterment of the program.

This leads me to a theory I came up with. I call it the "What if?" syndrome.

After realizing the brutal truth and reality of this process, I introduced it to my wife and children. Later some friends, and now I am able to implement it in my professional career and the various organizations I belong too.

The "What If?" syndrome is applied as such: In discussing with another decisionmaker, I asked myself, what if what that person is saying is correct or best? I don't have to agree or disagree with it, but what if it is true? How can I apply that action at that moment or in my life?

Now reflect on that for a moment. At this moment, it's not about you. What if what the other person is saying could be true? Without emotion, or retribution, how could what they are saying be applied for good? For the betterment of your relationship, the situation, the cause, for the betterment of everyone?

Imagine if we all could just sit back and ask, "What if?" about anything, any subject matter, and circumstance. How would all of us act towards each other, if we set emotion, biases, and territories aside?

There is "HOPE."
God does give "HOPE."

CHAPTER 11

Hope for Life

"Because I have been given much, I too must give."
—famous hymn

Through my healing journey, I discovered the desire and the need to help others in the similar situations that I was in.

I have always had a desire to serve others in the community, which came with a sense of self- accomplishment and a continued desire to give back. From a young age I knew I had to give back to those without a father, and those who lacked the people who stepped up to be leaders, mentors, and parental figures in my life.

The Hope for Life Foundation

As I started to write this book, I was continually reminded of my journey, the people and resources I was able to find, that enabled and empowered me to be confident and successful. Through this process, I kept getting this urge and inspiration to do more. There had to be a way and an organization that could reach out to Veterans and other men with a sense of restoring confidence and offering resources that could help them heal from the inside and improve their spiritual healing, mental well being, physical empowerment, and financial confidence. An organization that Veterans can reach out to and feel comfortable, knowing that they can relate to them.

How did the foundation come to be?

I remember having a distinct inspiration of what needed to be done, and what I had to do. My wife had the same feeling. I shared my thoughts with her, and we both concluded that we needed to start The Hope for Life Foundation. I reached out to some men I trusted and saw the vision as I did, to create the founding board.

The Hope for Life Foundation, a non-profit organization, is committed to assisting U.S. military veterans and their families to become confident, contributing members of their communities by strengthening their core, and gaining depth and meaning through their relationship with divinity. Enabling and empowering veterans to become confident contributing citizens in their communities.

Veterans of all military branches have a unique perspective on life. They have sacrificed much for a cause in which they unselfishly believe, and in the process most have gained knowledge and skills that can benefit employers, their families, and society in general. However, veterans often have a very difficult time re-engaging with "normal life," due to numerous factors including the vast difference between civilian life and military life, civilians' (including especially the veteran's family members) inability to understand the military life and its impact on the veteran, veterans' inability to "remember" what it is like to be a contributing civilian, and acute and prolonged traumatic events both in the veterans life and the lives of the veteran's families. These factors, and others, often lead to PTSD, depression, heightened anxiety, and suicide. Suicide rates among veterans are the highest of any group. The question, "How do we help a veteran become a confident, contributing citizen in their community," has been the focus of our efforts in The Hope for Life Foundation.

Many organizations have been organized to benefit veterans, but in most cases their approach tends to be focused on the short-term. In many cases, they invite a veteran on a hunt, fishing trip, or similar event presumably with the belief that this will constitute healing time. Unfortunately, this can only be a very temporary patch on the emotional wounds of a veteran who is suffering and it completely ignores the needs of the family of the veteran, which is often suffering just as much, but in different ways. Husbands and wives left at home need their spouses back with them fully. Children need their fathers and mothers back fully. Veterans need to feel accomplished in their roles in the home AND in society.

It is the Hope for Life Foundation's unshakeable belief that this can only be accomplished through God's help and by assisting the veteran and their family to connect with God, on a non-denominational basis, more fully and letting this healing influence bring the family back together, rendering the veteran a better leader in the home, which will then flow toward that veteran being a better leader in the community.

Hope for Life takes a multi-faceted approach. The first phase for each veteran is an intense 44-hour "retreat/seminar" in which the veteran will come face-to- face with their own relationship with God, and will be expected to set certain goals aimed toward their personal growth, their family's needs, and their role in society. Hope for Life will follow up with the veteran over time with these goals through a mix of ongoing weekend retreats, phone and video calls with mentors, and application of their assembled resources of experts to assist in aspects of the needs of the veterans. These experts may include individuals and organizations specializing in the areas of: resume building, employment search, work/life balance, psychological and therapeutic help, mortgage and financial professionals, clergy, family coping skills, fitness and dietary experts, marriage counselors, VA claims and appeals specialists, veterans organizations such as VFW, and American Legion.

Beyond this, we understand that a sense of accomplishment in small and large tasks and skills builds a person's confidence, leading to greater emotional stability and the ability to contribute to others. Therefore, as an integral part of the in-person portion of its programs, Hope for Life will provide activities and training in in variety of skills that many veterans tend to enjoy, including outdoor survival and bushcraft, ancient skills (such as blacksmithing, pottery, leatherwork, etc.), outdoor activities like fishing, hunting, camping, climbing, scuba, and other skills as indicated by our clients through an interest survey.

Following the veteran's engagement in the program, we will actively bring in the veteran's spouse and children, developing a program designed to lead them toward a similar path of devotion to God and service to mankind. This will culminate in weekend and week-long programs, Families of Hope Retreats, at Hope for Life's headquarter and satellite properties, designed as family camps. We envision not only a one-time family camp, but that families will be able to take advantage of our ongoing camps to make it a family tradition, creating the memories necessary to pull the veterans and their families through the tough times in life. This could extend in the future to more extensive family activities, like cruises.

Although we plan and HOPE to have the ability to offer sizable scholarships to our veterans and their families for our courses and programs, we expect each veteran to "buy in" with some investment. This can be in the form of cash payment toward their experience or labor/contribution toward the Hope for Life facilities and programs. Toward this, we will develop fundraising opportunities through which the veteran and their families will be able to actively support the mission of Hope for Life, as well as fund their own activities. These opportunities will additionally make the veterans' extended families, friends, and contacts in the wider community aware of their efforts and of the Hope for Life Foundation's mission and programs, thus increasing our reach.

Our key management team consists of veterans and those closely associated with our cause. Our CEO is a Navy veteran and very successful senior executive with Procter & Gamble. Our COO is an Army veteran, with an MBA, and having practiced high-level corporate law for many years. Our Chief Programs Officer has been the CFO of a major local company for many years, and our CFO is an expert in economics and finance. Another member of the team has been engaged in public affairs for many years and is extremely effective in getting the written word out to large audiences. We could go on. In short, we have the human capital to succeed in this venture.

We HOPE you will join with us in converting the amazing, and most often underutilized, resource of our nation's military veterans into the most dynamic beneficial resource in our communities, states, nation, and the world.

Events and Resources

- 44 hour Veteran faith strengthening experience with integrated goal-centered follow-up;
- 44 hour family based strengthening experience with integrated goal-centered follow-up;
- Week-long family summer camps - Families of Hope Retreats;
- Suicide Prevention seminars;
- Personal therapy counseling…. mental health and marriage counseling;
- Vocational Success support;
- Personal success coaching and seminars;
- Personal strength-based coaching;
- Community outings to local attractions, scenic rides, hunts, and other outdoor sporting activities;
- Informational and educational support for Veterans, and their families;
- Peer groups and community partnerships offering Veteran social engagement opportunities;
- Time spent with fellow Veterans, and other professionals in social service fields;
- Service opportunities for Veterans and their families; and
- Trained professional staff.

For more details, please visit our website and follow our Facebook page. Be sure to get the audio version of this book so you can listen while you drive, workout, and at other times of your day.

Website: www.thehopeforlife.org
Facebook: https://www.facebook.com/TheHopeForLifeFoundation
Ways to donate:
   Venmo: @TheHopeForLife-2021
   PayPal: Hope For Life

CHAPTER 12

The Empowerment Journey

When you believe in people, care about them,
and trust them, they know it.
—*Blair D. Hope*

In the end, it took all that I went through, all those experiences, and trials to make me the man I am today. This has me doing a lot of thinking and reflecting. I would like to share some thoughts with you. These thoughts are not all about me, but about the teams and the results that they have enjoyed.

I have often been asked how do you do it, or why do you do it that way? How did you survive your childhood? How did you become the youngest Petty Officer in the Navy? How did you receive those accommodation awards? How did you get hired by Procter & Gamble with no college degree? How can you lead the country in sales within P&G? How did you get 78 Venture Boy Scouts to your activity? How did you get recognized for recruiting the most Wood Badge participants in a year? How did you re-charter 100 percent on time for three years as a BSA District Commissioner? How did you attend Philmont Training Center as a participant one year and then get asked to come back and be an instructor the next year? How did you raise $4,000-6,000 from the Order of the Arrow (OA) Scout Memorabilia and Trade-O-Ree Auction? How are you getting 15 young men to attend your OA chapter activities? How did you get six people to get registered for Coup Trail? How did you get 16 people registered for Section Conclave?

I am able to accomplish these things because I was empowered to do so. But most importantly, I empower others to do so. I think it is important to remember that you should always start with the end in mind. From there you figure out how to get there. Everything I do is based on **relationships**, networking, enabling, and empowerment.

What does it mean to empower others?

There are qualifications you must have, or pursue, to be able to effectively empower others. As you empower others they will then empower you when they respond to you in a positive way.

Position

You must have a position of leadership. You cannot empower people if you don't lead. Only a person in authority can give another person permission to succeed. Others can encourage, but permission comes only from an authority figure.

Relationship

It's all about relationships. "A great man shares his greatness by the way he treats little men." Although the people you can empower are not "little," they can be made to feel that way if you don't value your relationship with them. Relationships are forged, not formed.

Respect

Relationships cause people to want to be with you, but respect causes people to want to be empowered by you. Mutual respect is essential in the empowerment process. Everyone wants to feel like he counts for something and is important to someone. If you wish others to respect you, you must show respect for them. Invariably, people will give their love, respect, and attention to the person who fills that need. Consideration for others generally reflects faith in oneself and faith in others.

When you believe in people, care about them, and trust them, they know it. And that respect inspires them to want to follow where you lead.

Commitment

The process of empowering others isn't easy. It can be difficult and rough along the way. But it is worth the journey because the rewards are so great. People must believe that a task is inherently worthwhile if they are to be committed to it. When you empower people, you're not influencing just them, you're influencing all the people they influence. That's impact!

If you have authority in people's lives, have built relationships with them, respect them, and have committed yourself to the process of empowerment, you are in a position to empower them. But that's not all. There is one more crucial element of empowering that needs to take place. You must have the right attitude. Attitude is 10 percent what happens to you and 90 percent how you react to it.

Many people neglect to empower others because they are insecure. They are afraid of losing their jobs to the people they mentor. They feel threatened. They don't want to be replaced or displaced, even if it means that they would be able to move up the ladder to a higher position and leave their current position only to be filled by the person they mentor. I call that **True Success**. They are afraid of change. But change is part of empowerment – for the people you empower and for yourself. If you want to go up, there are things you have to be willing to give up.

Questions to ask yourself along the empowerment journey:

1. Do I believe in people and feel that they are my organization's most appreciable asset?

2. Do I believe that empowering others can accomplish more than individual achievement?

3. Do I actively search for leaders to empower?

4. Would I be willing to raise others to a level higher than my own level of leadership?

5. Would I be willing to invest time developing people who have leadership potential?

6. Would I be willing to let others get credit for what I taught them?

7. Do I allow others freedom of personality and process, or do I have to be in control?

8. Would I be willing to publicly give my authority and influence to potential leaders?

9. Would I be willing to hand the leadership baton to the people I empower and truly root for them?

How do I empower others.

Once you have confidence in yourself and in the people you wish to empower, you're ready to begin the process. The goal would be to hand over relatively small, simple tasks in the beginning and progressively increase their responsibilities and authority.

1. Evaluate them
   a) Their knowledge
   b) Their Skill
   c) Their Desire

2. Model for them
   Even people with knowledge, skill, and desire need to know what's expected of them, and the best way to inform them is to show them. People do what people see. Are you the chicken or the Eagle?

3. Give them permission to succeed.
   You have to help others believe that they can succeed and show them that you want them to succeed. How do you do that?
   o Expect it.
   o Verbalize it.
   o Reinforce it.

Once people recognize and understand that you genuinely want to see them succeed and are committed to helping them, they will begin to believe they can accomplish what you give them to do.

4. Transfer authority to them.

      The real heart of empowerment is to transfer your authority and influence to the people you are mentoring and developing. Many people are willing to give others responsibility. They gladly delegate tasks to them. But empowering others is more than sharing your workload. It's sharing your power and ability to get things done.

5. Publicly show your confidence in them.

6. Supply them with feedback.

7. Release them to continue on their own.

What are the results of empowerment?

Reproduction and Multiplication
The Power of Multiplication:
- Reproducing leaders raises your influence to a new level.
- Reproducing leaders raises the new
- leaders' potential.
- Reproducing leaders multiplies resources.
- Reproducing leaders ensures a positive future for your organization.

How do you awaken the reproducer within you?

- Lead yourself well.
- Look continually for potential leaders.
- Put the Team first

Ask yourself:

1. Do I add value to others?
2. Do I add value to the organization?
3. Am I quick to give away the credit when things go right?

4. Is our team consistently adding new members?
5. Do I use my "bench" players as much as I should?
6. Do many people on the team consistently make important decisions?
7. Is our team's emphasis on creating victories more than just producing stars?

SHARE OF MIND – How often will others think of your vision and goals when you are not there?

You need to commit yourself to developing leaders, not followers.

If we do not succeed in these most important questions, we will lose great young men and adults. They will be siphoned into other organizations and activities where they feel self-worth and acceptance. We need to help them survive through a synergetic program and most importantly, we need to create a significance.

I was empowered to do great things. It is more empowering to enable others to do more great things! **"The reward of a job well done, is to have done it."**

Sometimes it takes the whole journey to realize you are somebody, you are a Son of God, you do have a purpose in this life. You can influence others. You can build the confidence you need.

How it all comes together is quite the wonder.

So I ask you:

"Is there HOPE?"
YES
"GOD DOES GIVE HOPE!"

In a very humbling way, God gave the world "ME," and I have empowered YOU!

"I am HOPE" and I have given that HOPE to YOU. Now go and DO!

ABOUT THE AUTHOR

Blair D. Hope served in the U.S. Navy, started several companies, led large corporate sales teams, and is known for his "outside of the box" thinking. When presented with obstacles in his path, Blair leads with one of his favorite sayings, "Don't let challenges stump you, provide the opportunity." When others told him that he could not do it, he found a way and set records! He has sold millions of dollars in products and contracts, and has successfully coached, mentored, and led dozens of businesses and volunteer organizations. Blair has overcome adversity, disability, depression, and PTSD. He strives to enable and empower others.

He has received many awards and achievements and has had leadership and adventures in 33 states and 14 countries. He has been recognized as a national sales leader with the Center of Excellence Award from Procter & Gambel, awarded to only the top 5 percent in the company. He has been globally recognized for his leadership in the Boy Scouts of America as a volunteer. He has business degrees from Chapman University and Utah State University.

Blair is a feature film actor, a professional speaker and trainer, as well as a business expert. After completing this book, he is currently working on his second and third books.

He has extensive experience in many facets of leadership, mentoring, management, and business. He has directed the start-up of three businesses. His ability to network while finding the passion and talent of others is immeasurable. Blair is the founder and CEO of the non- profit organization "The Hope for Life Foundation," Proudly serving veterans.

Blair has become a distinguished Scouter, leader, businessman, author, consultant, and mentor. He has served in several leadership positions for the County and State legislation. He has been a Keynote speaker, and motivator for several national training courses. He has enjoyed local and district leadership positions with Kiwanis International. He thrives on building better men through Masonry.

He has taught and coached on local, regional, and national levels. He has been a delegate to report to the state level on youth programs. Blair has chosen to actively learn and participate in the many roles of business to be well rounded to fit the varying demands of executive leadership. In 2014 he was nationally recognized for his Scouting leadership, being presented with the National Outstanding Eagle Scout Award. Blair is an Ambassador of Scouting and has traveled around the country to teach youth and adults how to improve their lives through solid principles and skills.

Blair Hope was born and raised in Utah. His family traveled when he was an infant due to his father being in the Army. Blair is married to his beautiful wife Christine, and they have six wonderful children. Together they have celebrated 28 years of marriage and many other milestones. Blair served eight years in the United States Navy as an Aircraft Handler and Naval Aviation Warfare Specialist. His military career included combat experience and operations in Kuwait, Desert Storm, Desert Shield, Iraq and Africa. Blair is employed as an executive with Procter & Gamble for the past 20 years. Blair lives by a motto and a vision, "Don't let challenges stump you, provide the opportunity" and "What do you want your legacy to look like?"

ACKNOWLEDGMENTS

This book has been a dream of mine for some time, but the lack of confidence held it back from coming to fruition for many years.

To those who have mentored me, guided me, and participated in all my adventures, I salute you.

To all the mother and father figures who stepped up and looked after me, especially Myrna Jackson, Barbara Carr, Tom Jackson, and Dave Isom.

To my best friend, Andy Jackson, for asking the new kid if he wanted to walk home with him instead of walking alone. For being a great example, for his unconditional patience and friendship.

To all the Scout Masters and leaders who took the time to care and develop a young boy and showed him he was not alone.

To all the military leaders for their unrelentless structure, attention to detail, accountability, and responsibility.

To my grandfather, Parley Albert Sargent, for taking me in and not giving up on me. For being a great example of what success looks like. He said: "Success is the number of people at your bedside when you pass away."

To all of those who feel there is no hope and feel the lack of confidence, "There is Hope."

And finally, to Dave Bresnahan for his endless hours of editing and guiding me through the writing process of this book. Thank you!

www.ingramcontent.com/pod-product-compliance
Lightning Source LLC
Chambersburg PA
CBHW031220120626
46545CB00003B/928